One Witch's Way

About the Author

Bronwynn Forrest Torgerson is a prolific writer who has been a solitary Witch for many years. She has contributed to *Circle*, *SageWoman*, and *Widdershins* magazines, in addition to creating the Pagan networking newsletters she publishes and distributes.

Bronwynn lives in Glendale, Arizona, where for several years she has been one of the principal organizers of Phoenix's Pagan Pride Day. She is co-chair of the speaker's bureau for Valley of the Sun Pagan Projects and is a member of the Covenant of Unitarian Universalist Pagans (CUUPS). Bronwynn frequently presents lay-led services at West Valley Unitarian Universalist Church, where Wiccans are welcome.

She served as submissions editor for the Pagan Arizona Network and was the galvanizing force behind the Central Illinois Pagan Alliance. Bronwynn remains active in her faith community and is available to assist in the creation of handfastings, memorials, and customized rites of passage.

Please visit Bronwynn's website at http://www.thebronwynn.com.

To Write to the Author

If you wish to contact the author or would like more information about this book, please write to the author in care of Llewellyn Worldwide and we will forward your request. Both the author and publisher appreciate hearing from you and learning of your enjoyment of this book and how it has helped you. Llewellyn Worldwide cannot guarantee that every letter written to the author can be answered, but all will be forwarded. Please write to:

Bronwynn Forrest Torgerson
℅ Llewellyn Worldwide
2143 Wooddale Drive, Dept. 978-0-7387-1369-4
Woodbury, MN 55125-2989, U.S.A.

Please enclose a self-addressed stamped envelope for reply,
or $1.00 to cover costs. If outside the U.S.A., enclose an
international postal reply coupon.

Many of Llewellyn's authors have websites with additional information and resources. For more information, please visit our website at http://www.llewellyn.com.

BRONWYNN FORREST TORGERSON

ONE
WITCH's WAY

A MAGICAL YEAR OF

STORIES,

SPELLS

& SUCH

Llewellyn Publications
Woodbury, Minnesota

First Edition
First Printing, 2008

Book design by Steffani Sawyer
Editing by Brett Fechheimer
Cover design by Kevin R. Brown
Cover images of birdhouse and wheat © 2008 by BrandX Pictures
Llewellyn is a registered trademark of Llewellyn Worldwide, Ltd.

Library of Congress Cataloging-in-Publication Data for *One Witch's Way: A Magical Year of Stories, Spells & Such* is on file at the Library of Congress.

ISBN: 978-0-7387-1369-4

Llewellyn Publications
A Division of Llewellyn Worldwide, Ltd.
2143 Wooddale Drive, Dept. 978-0-7387-1369-4
Woodbury, Minnesota 55125-2989, U.S.A.
www.llewellyn.com

Printed in the United States of America

To the Great Gray Man who walks at my side
and possesses the power of "What if?"

In this birthing of my first book, I give endless thanks . . .

To Elaine Foxwell, a warrior woman whose editor's sword helped cleave away the dross in my work and expose the veins of gold. To Daniel Merlyn Poland, my soulmate husband, who rubbed my back and listened to me whimper when I discovered how intensive the publishing process truly is. How great shall be his reward!

I am grateful to my sisters Marilyn and Ruth for believing in me from the start, and to Amy who reminded me that one must walk through fire to get to the other side. My family, both of blood and of the heart, frame my existence and I cherish Angela, Kevin, Arthur, Andi, Kristen, and Moraelyn. I raise a cup to Kathy and Ann, to those feisty crones of Witch's Moon, and to my brothers and sisters of the Craft, both known and still to be met. Lastly, I celebrate Autumn and Joad, whose love is the loom on which some of my best ritual weaving has been done. How brightly your threads do shine in the tapestry of my life!

Contents

Foreword

Dear reader,

The title of this book, *One Witch's Way*, is both a directional arrow and a declaration. Although we may all derive inspiration from many sources, after all the books have been replaced on our shelves and the acclaimed lecturers have turned out the lights and gone home, we are ultimately each "one Witch" making magic in our own way. How each of us will individually respond when a phone call comes in the wee hours that necessitates an energy working, or when the need of the moment is now, depends on our circumstances and what lies at hand. A wizard once asked his apprentice, "Whose hand contains the magic?" The answer, of course, is your own. Whatever works for you is valid.

In each month-themed chapter of *One Witch's Way*, you will find a trio of rituals or workings designed to help you tap into the empowering energy of that time of year. I have not included celebrations for any of the major sabbats, as those already exist in great profusion. Rather, it is my privilege to share my original rites of passage, transcendence, liberation, acknowledgement, and joy. I hope that within these pages you will find something to love, to ponder, and ultimately to adapt as your own.

I tried really hard, while word weaving this book, to leave my personal narrative out. Then I realized that just as you, my reader, are one Witch, so am I. I wanted you to know me. I longed to share my stories, and somewhere down the road I look forward to hearing your own. All paths converge at some point, and I am glad we are sharing this journey to one Witch's way together . . .

Old Ones bless!

October

November

December

January
all about journeys

February

March

April

May

June

July

August

September

Awakenings

I danced with the Maiden upon the lea.
She turned her fearless gaze on me,
Said, "There's so much you've never been
You still could be. Have you been caged,
Or do you walk free . . . ?"
Race with the old gods,
Run through the night!
Reach for the power,
Reclaim the right!
The Mother came down a sweet green lane
With cakes and daffodils.
She said, "Through Beltane's blossoms
Is Imbolc's pledge made real.
Some regret the youth that was spent;
Tell me, are you fulfilled?"
Sing to the old gods,
Sing through the night.
Pray for the courage
To finish the fight.
I called the Crone one night alone,
We talked for quite a while.
She said, "You've done okay, kid;
I rather like your style."
Then grew the Hag more pensive,
I heard her heave a sigh . . .
"Why is it man cannot understand,
You must live before you die?"
Soar with the old gods
So brilliant and bright!
Burn like a comet
With no end in sight!

Although we of the Craft honor Samhain on October 31st as the old year passing and the new one just begun, the calendar on the wall still guides our life. In January we look out over the uncharted landscape of another year: pristine, full of promise, potential, hopefully prosperity and success—but inevitably changes, too. In January we reflect on where we wish to be living this time next year. We look back over the auto payments and repair bills, and consider whether it may be time for a worthier steed. We plan how to get from point A to point B. We take stock of our lives.

In this chapter, those readers who are longing for a home to call their own will find a way to call it into being and to claim and bless it when it appears. There are charms to ensure your car's safety on the road and a method of releasing your four-wheeled steed when a new one would serve you better. Come share my journey, dear reader, as you embark on adventures of your own. Let us begin.

There's No Place Like Home

Although spring is far from sprung, your nesting urge has begun. Tired of living in cramped quarters with insufficient closet space to store your ritual robes? No room for your cauldron collection or latest stockpile of herbs? Then perhaps it's time to find a new place to hang your pointy hat. Roll up those witchy sleeves and let's get cracking.

Here is a lighthearted and airy house-finding and house-blessing ritual for people who know in their bones that it's time to seek out a home of their own. You've long outgrown your parents' nest and passed the nomadic apartment-dweller phase. The new you longs for stability and a place to call home. You want your name on a mailbox, invitations to loathsome homeowner's association meetings. You covet a mantel on which to display Grandma Madison's china or Grandpa Rossman's musket. You yearn for trees you can get to know over many seasons and neighbors you can count on, and you have your resources all in a row. This home-finding ritual can help sharpen the focus and bring your dream house into the land of manifest reality.

Do your mundane homework first. Check the listings and property values, listen up for real estate agents that are real wizards at cinching a deal and taking your priorities to heart. Then enter the magical realms . . .

Calling Your Home to You

You will need a bird's nest, a hollowed-out dried egg that you can write on with a fine-point marking pen, a gold candle, an object or drawing to symbolize your house, a piece of parchment paper, and a small but sturdy fire to be laid of straw and twigs. Warning: shakest thou not the nests from the trees but go ye into craft stores instead, where such things in great bounty await!

Make a simple altar outdoors and decorate it with those things important to your tradition. For the representation of your house, many possibilities exist. Do you own a Monopoly set? Pluck a green plastic house from the box. Have a Yule decoration shaped like a gingerbread house? That will do fine. You can also simply draw a house outline on the parchment paper, leaving room for your list of specs. Don't worry if it's not perfect—love and the Universe will make it so. On the egg, write "My new home." You can add your name, date, and runes or other magical sigils if you want.

Now comes your shopping list. Be as specific as you can, while keeping a healthy amount of realism in play. Where should the house be in relation to work, school, culture, family, and so on? Envision your ideal floor plan, describing it in words. Is there a yard? A garden space? Is it environmentally friendly? How big is the garage? What would you like within strolling distance? For price range, you might want to give two figures: the first being what you'd prefer to pay and the second being the highest you can go.

When you are done, roll up your parchment paper into a scroll thin enough to be inserted through the open ends of the hollowed egg. Where else would a dream house hatch? Cast circle in your way, lastly lighting the gold candle and invoking your patron deity, or whomever you feel most likely to help you in this rite. You may wish to call upon the Goddess in her guise as Bird Goddess, ancient Mother of us all, from whom the egg of the world was laid. Other hearth fire keepers might include Juno, Vesta, Brigit, or Hestia. Nordic types may turn to Frigga as queen mother of Asgard, or even to good friend Thor, known to gladly bless a new stead and to party with the best.

A suggested invocation might be:

"By the spark within my breast,
Feel my longing for a nest.
Grant that I, contented, dwell
By sacred words and ancient spell
So mote it be!"

Holding the egg cupped in your hands, speak aloud your dearest wishes and desires for your home, including the time frame in which you hope to find it. Kiss the egg gently and lay it in the nest, thanking Deity for making it hatch with all-knowing magic. Lay the nest atop the twigs and straw you will use to kindle the fire, then light the spark. As the nest and egg burn, know that your mental blueprints are rising to the heavens where your Hallowed House Hunter is seeing them clearly and already beginning to discern where your perfect home might be.

Close circle in your way, but allow the gold candle to burn out. If that is not possible all in one night, pinch it out and relight it for the next several nights until the candle is gone.

Get yourself a cardboard box and pack some unneeded things away. This signals the Universe that you are becoming mobile and can take occupancy of your new home as soon as the closing documents are signed.

House Blessing Ritual

Huzzah! The Old Ones and your banker have come shining through! You dance a wild jig, sign a million papers, and are petrified and exhilarated. You are now a homeowner!

The first new moon after you have keys in hand and have unpacked enough things to live sanely from day to day, invite friends over to bless your new home. Ask each to bring you a coin from the happiest place they have visited recently so that your home might be blessed with joy and abundance, and a bell to ring for mirth and to summon the fey folk forth. Provide an attractive crystal dish or clear bowl to hold the coins.

Light a white taper candle and trace an invoking pentagram at every entrance, asking that truth, benevolence, and harmony enter in. You may wish to add an extra wish for great sex, creativity, personal growth and new opportunities, or other heart's desires. Hand your favorite blessing oil to a special friend and have them bless each reflective surface by drawing the same invoking pentagram in oil and expressing the same wish. Burn some sage or your favorite magical incense, inviting all unseen creatures of goodly heart and helpful hands to come and dwell therein.

After this is accomplished, guests may deposit their coins one by one into the dish, telling of the happy place in which the coin made its way into their pockets. Never spend these coins, but rather look upon this hoard as treasure of the heart and a certain guarantee that you will never be impoverished.

Those guests who have bells now go merrily ringing and dancing through the place, proclaiming lighthearted wishes for you as they do so: "I wish for your cat to love it here! I wish you incredibly lusty romps! May nothing you cook in this kitchen ever burn! May there always be wine in your fridge!" Let unbounded imagination bring forth creative, graphic, heartfelt, and humorous wishes. Well-wishers may shout "Huzzah!" or "So mote it be!"

Find the heart of your house. You will feel it when you walk through the door. Is it under the ceiling fan in the living room? Near the kitchen table? Go there now and take your friends along. It is time to claim your home, sharing with it your hopes and rightful praise.

Ask several guests to join in. Create a blessing charm and give a portion to each friend to read aloud. You can print words ahead of time on colored index cards and once they are read, retain them as a housewarming keepsake. Say something like this:

"This is a marvelous house!
With friends in every chair
And love beyond compare.
This is a wonderful house!
This is a blessed house!
Prosperity abounds
And hearty laughter sounds.
This is a loving house!
This is a magical house!
Health, wealth, good fortune, too.
All blessings come to you.
May there be such joy in this house!"

This would be the perfect time for a toast to you, to the God/Goddess, to your new home, and to many years of happiness together. Congratulations!

Magic for Rent, Inquire Within

I once manifested a lovely tower apartment in this fashion. With the Y2K scare looming only a few months ahead, I made my shopping list: The place must be utterly safe, with a protected entry and in a well-policed neighborhood. On my tiny budget, utilities must be included. The apartment must be large enough for me and my things and (the impossible part) cost less than $300 per month. Friends promised to help me move but shook their heads and chided me for being so naïve as to expect "all that."

Two weeks later, a friend phoned who knew the owner of a property in an historic district in town. It was originally a mansion, dating back to the 1890s, previously home to a wealthy spiritualist named Dorothy. It was purchased soon after her death by one who had loved her in life. It was said that on the day Dorothy left this plane, every blackbird in town touched down on the lawn and waited to carry her over. Might I wish to inquire? Write down this number then.

I drove to the towering brick and stained-glass building, now housing an architectural firm and with a separate studio apartment hidden somewhere inside. I explored the grounds a bit, and was charmed to find wooden black cat silhouettes adorning the gates and enormous cauldron-shaped planters in the back! If they didn't want to attract a Witch, they shouldn't have put out bait!

One whole wing belonged to the property managers. Stern old Mr. Radnowski scoured my references and deigned to accept my check. Then his good-hearted wife Valentina led me to the little round bell tower, smack in the third-floor peak of the place. To gain entry, one either had to get by fiery-eyed, gun-toting Radnowski at the front door or climb the Himalayan fire escape.

The tower proved to be a multiroom studio with whimsical quirks. Heat was provided, and the air conditioner ran on quarters. A tiny coin slot meter, in a gnome-sized closet under the eaves, got you four hours for twenty-five cents. Because of the high ceilings and drafty windows, bats dropped in from time to time. Rainbows appeared in photos I took in the bedroom. I thanked Dorothy frequently for her hospitality. Her portrait still hangs in the office of the place, and I know her spirit hovers to make sure all guests are respectful.

Radnowski, bless his crotchety soul, turned a blind eye when my friend, the yard sale queen, packed my mailbox with rummage sale Halloween brooms. The price of this magical bastion? $295.00 per month.

Vehicular Protection Spells

Here is some simple spellwork that can make motoring a whole lot easier. As I turn the key each morning, I trace an invisible pentagram over my steering wheel, chanting:

> "Spell and magic, three times three
> Swift, safe journeys grant to me
> That I might reach my destination
> Without accident, incident or cops (unless I need them).
> So mote it be and blessed be!"

When parking in an unlit area, or in a place where vandalism has been known to occur, trace an invoking pentagram on your front and back windshields, and driver and passenger-side windows, saying:

> "Spell and magic, three times three
> Guard thou well what belongs to me!
> Stand guard and sentry while I'm gone,
> Let this magic spell wear on!
> So mote it be!"

Stuck in snail's-pace traffic? After you've colorfully cussed a bit, simmer down. Wave your power hand back and forth in an undulating motion. Repeat:

> "Ebb and flow, ebb and flow
> Swiftly, safely on you go!"

Things should begin to move again.

Turning over the Wheel

The time will come when you decide to relinquish your wheels and trade them for a better besom. Many of us imbue our four-wheeled friends with personalities, names, praise, and pleas. We coax them to crank over in the mornings and beseech them to coast a few more blocks to the cheapest gas station on the day before payday. You aren't pawning off an impersonal object. You're preparing to part with a mechanical friend.

Thank your car, truck, or SUV for the service it has given to you. As unobtrusively as possible, walk clockwise around your vehicle, carrying a lit stick of incense or a pinch of smoldering sage. At its eastern sphere, thank the vehicle aloud for all the splendid sunrises and sunsets you saw while driving it. At the south, thank it for the enthusiasm you felt, taking off on a weekend camp-out, rummage sale or road trip, and for its trusty spark of ignition in getting you there and back. At the west, speak your gratitude for the feelings your travels have evoked in you—the joys of seeing old friends again, the solemnity of attending an unexpected wake, wherever life has taken you. Finally, at the north, think back on all the seasons this car has served you. Praise its loyalty and all the miles it gave you. Release it from its allegiance to you, and free it to be purchased by another. I did these things and signed over my car title to a new owner the very same night. Safe journeys to you and yours along the highway of life.

Three Years and Out . . . How Odin Led the Way

What god shall we say charts our journeys? What cartographer lays out the course? In 1988 my wanderings led me from my native Illinois to Phoenix, Arizona. A starving single parent then, wincing when the winter heating bill arrived, I reasoned that being warm and poor in Arizona might be better. My twin son and daughter were turning twelve and up for the adventure.

Though my love of sacred places and geology first led me to Arizona on a college field trip when my children were very young, the desert has never been my home. The part of Arizona that originally swept away my senses was the Indian country, north of Flagstaff. A voice spoke to me in the wind at the ruins of Wupatki. A spirit face peered through a deerskin stretched on a birch frame at the craggy monument of Tuzi-goot. Friends lived in Phoenix, however, and promised aid in finding jobs and an apartment, and so we came. My daughter married her high school sweetheart and made a life in Arizona. My son mourned trees and seasons and returned to Illinois.

In November 1997 I was ready to head northwest. Arizona had given me both blessings and heartaches. I had found Craft community, whereas in Illinois I'd been "the only unicorn in town." In Arizona I had edited a Pagan newsletter, hosted open sabbats and full moon circles, and met a myriad of magical souls. I had also known the acrid taste of love's illusion and despair, and it would be quite awhile before I opened my heart again.

I heard the call of Puget Sound and knew healing awaited me there. My gaze had fallen on Bellingham, Washington, up against the Canadian border. Tall cedars, draped in tendrils of fairy hair moss, had secrets to share with me. Puget Sound, in its mystery, awaited, and Raven watched for me. I longed for a home I had never known.

I closed out my bank account, gave notice on my apartment and my job, and started packing boxes. Then came the calls from Illinois, from my now-grown son who shared an apartment with my widowed dad. "I took Grandpa to the emergency room last night, Mom," one phone message said. The next day the report was better, then back to ER again. I had visited my father a couple of months before all this began, and he was his usual quirky, happily-fishing-and-tinkering self then. This downhill pattern was disturbing and as my father's only child, I didn't know what to do.

Brain trauma from an accident in his youth had rendered my father mentally unstable since the age of twelve. While delivering papers by bicycle, he was hit by a passing car. Dad lay in a coma for several days before regaining consciousness. In lucid times, my father cracked jokes, fished and hunted with buddies from work. During his darker days, he would grow delusional, violent, accusatory, and perverse.

My dad in his seventh decade was good to my son. My own childhood, however, was filled with calls to the police, fist-fights between my folks, and objects thrown and shattered. My mother and I hoarded Christmas presents and tried to sneak Christmas past my father's brooding glare and the threat of his eruption at any time. After my mother's death in '87, I filed a quit claim deed on my childhood home, giving sole ownership back to my dad who quickly sold it off. I moved to Arizona and no birthday cards or Christmas greetings followed me. Except for my phone calls, which he was usually too busy to accept, my dad and I had distanced. A forgotten daughter I had become. Now the man's days were numbered, and a hard decision lay in my hands.

I called together a circle, summoning the least fanciful folks I knew. I didn't need "dragons in the clouds" or sage interpretations from anyone else. I needed the plain, hard truth. Four freshly filled canister-style torches flanked the four directions. I flung my atlas open to the map of the entire United States on the ground in the middle. Circle was cast and quarters called, and then I held up my hands to the heavens and declared to Hecate, "I stand here at the crossroads. One road calls to the depths of my heart, another road calls to my kin. Where would you have me go?"

The flame on the torch in the east shot up four inches, while the other three simultaneously dimmed. It was like someone had thrown a switch. The answer could not be questioned. I was to return to Illinois. With a heart like lead and a bellyful of sorrow, I closed circle and went home. I cursed and cried, knowing my obligation and hating it all the while. "Don't you strand me there!" I ranted to the gods, my voice hoarse. The Illinois I'd left behind had been conservative, Christian, and condemning of anyone different. "Don't you make me stay!" I cried.

A clairaudient answer came: "It's a three-year commitment."

"You had better not ask me to stay there one day longer!" I wailed.

"It's a three-year commitment," I heard again.

"How will I know when my time is up?" I wanted to know.

"We shall send someone to tell you."

The 1,700 miles sped easily away. I pulled into my father's driveway in November of '97, just as he was loading fishing poles into his rusty, rattletrap blue station wagon. He smoothed back his shock of unruly white hair and greeted me. "I'm seventy-three years old now. I'm living on borrowed time." I silently answered, "Yes, Dad, I know."

The following month he lay dead of a stomach aneurism. My son found him stretched out on the living room floor when he returned from working third shift. A memorial service was held, and none of his six widowed lady-friends clawed each other's eyes out or fought over Dad's cremains. Men in their seventies with a full head of hair and a running car were a hot commodity indeed, and his loss was felt by many.

On a bitterly cold December day, with the frozen ground jutting up into hard, sharp ridges underfoot, my son and I took Dad's ashes and scattered them riverside. I tidied up Dad's apartment, scraped dead earthworms out of the crisper, paid his remaining bills, settled his meager estate, and found myself excluded from his will: "For reasons known best to me and my daughter, I choose not to provide for her." My funds, accrued toward moving to Washington state, had slowly trickled out. And so I stayed, found work and my tower apartment, and reinforced ties with family and old friends.

Many job assignments took me past a Unitarian Universalist (known informally as UU) church, whose sayings in the glass-encased message board outside always hit uncannily home—my own private fortune cookie for how the week would go. Curiosity overcame me, and one Sunday morning I timidly stepped inside. The moment they lit the flaming chalice, uncannily like a cauldron, I was hooked. The following week I attended a full moon drumming circle in the church's basement fellowship room. It was already in progress when I tiptoed down the stairs and stood uncertainly hovering, not wishing to intrude. The minister rose and came over to me. "We saved you a seat," he said, waving his hand toward the one empty chair in the circle. "Won't you come join us, please."

Witches were welcome at the UU church. Spiritualists were, too. One afternoon, during a spiritualist message service, the old man reading for me squinted and furrowed his brow. "I see you with an instrument," he began, then concentrated more. "It's a musical instrument . . . what do you call those things? Ah . . . panpipes. I see you holding panpipes and wondering if it's safe to play them here. Yes, play the pipes. Many here are waiting to hear the tune."

I was soon enlisted in teaching a Wicca 101 course at that church. There I met Autumn and Joad. A hunger for magic does not go unfed for long. From that class sprang fledgling Moon Grove Coven, which later incarnated into the Central Illinois Pagan Alliance.

My series of Midwestern careers finally led me to a job at the front desk of an old, impoverished cemetery in receivership. Its honeycombed hills and wooded valleys sprawled out for six hundred acres. The mausoleum was haunted by a man seen standing barefoot in the snow. Raccoons had taken up residence, chewing their way through the back chambers of the decrepit office building. Plat books and interment records were hefty and dusty, with no data on computers. As the secretary, I searched records for genealogies, scheduled burials, and tried to sort out the broken heap of discarded monuments and markers piled around the back.

One day in the fall of 2000 a stout old man came shuffling through the door. He was retired and disabled, he said, and whittled walking sticks out of deadfall branches to supplement his income. He sold them at craft fairs and such. Would I write out a permission letter, he asked me, so that if anyone saw him picking up wood, they wouldn't give him a hard time? Sure, I said, charmed by his sincerity. Might I like a hiking stick myself, he asked. Seeing that he wanted to give something back, I said yes. Maybe a little acorn on the end? And could he wood-burn the bindrunes I drew, my runic initials, onto it? Easy enough, he nodded, and tucked my sketch in his pocket.

A week later he returned, my walking stick in hand. It was he and I, alone in the office, the other employees out servicing the grounds. I praised the carving on the staff, ran my fingers over the well-oiled shaft. "This is beautiful work, sir," I said.

The old man gazed intently into my eyes and then quietly asked, "Would you deceive a one-eyed man?" The room fell away and my skin rippled with goose bumps. The god Odin, in Wanderer guise, had chosen a human mount and walked right through that door.

"No, sir . . . I would not." I managed to gulp in reply.

He regarded me. "Why are you still here then? Your three years are up . . . " With that said, the room returned to normal, and there was just that plump old man and me. He examined my desktop rock collection, then went about his way.

The gods had kept their promise, and I had honored mine. My journey there was done.

If Your Car Tells You Its Name . . .

I've always named my four-wheeled steeds or, rather, listened for what they wished to be called. I laid my hand on the hood of my very first love, a 1974 beige Gremlin X, and knew it was Archimedes, just like Merlin's owl in *Sword in the Stone*. I put a million miles on that little fleet-winged beast, before laying it to rest.

Its successor was not so benevolent. I learned the hard way that hearing a car declare "I am Armageddon!" translates into "Do not buy me! Run fast!" That black and green Gremlin had been wrecked, rebuilt, and rewired by the teenage owner. Six weeks after the sale was made, it fried itself in the driveway. I watched the smoke curl up and thought to myself, "Damn! If I had only spoken Patriarchy!" If it had said, "Just call me Ragnarok," I would've understood.

Kalikrates, the electric-blue Pacer X, had a drinking problem. Every week it knocked back four quarts of oil and two quarts of transmission fluid just to keep it staggering down the street.

My present roadworthy friend declared, "I am the Bonny Blue!" to me soon after we met. I was not surprised to learn that flags and ships had also proudly borne that name. My blue-jay-colored Toyota sails gaily down the road and has a knack for joyful new discoveries. Listen for who your car declares itself to be.

> Proverb: If your hands are full of yesterday,
> how can they reach for tomorrow?

November

December

January

February
fans the flames

March

April

May

June

July

August

September

October

North Star

Be my North Star, ever guide me
No matter how far I may roam.
I'll never be lost if you're standing beside me,
For the light in your eyes will guide my way home.
Be my safe harbor, my refuge,
And I can survive any storm.
I'll weather the gale, though tattered the sail,
If I know in your arms I'll be warm.
Be my future, my something to cling to,
And my dreams I'll entrust to your care.
My heart says it's right to tell you tonight
That I want you to always be there . . .

fans the flames

february

February is all about fire—whether the flames of love as we open to another or the rosy glow of Spirit's forge as we enter Imbolc's time of initiation and transformation. As for the transition we undergo as we dedicate ourselves to a course of study, a pantheon, or a god, let me tell you of a dream a wizard shared with me long ago.

He dreamt himself surrounded by searing heat. Heavy blows rained on his back. The mage struggled and tried to wriggle free. Then a voice thundered down, "The sword will now lie still!" He didn't understand. Came the voice more quietly, "Do you not know how much force is required to forge a sword of steel, gleaming and powerful? You, and those like you, are swords in the hand of the gods." While my friend may have been pounded into perfection, my self-dedication ritual is gentler but full of beauty and meaning. Please join me as we emerge shining and new!

In perfect love, I offer to you one golden rose. It is the symbol of readiness and hope for communication, as strangers become friends and possibly more. The Sea Mother spell will tumble you like a stone, gently sanding away any jagged edges and leaving you shining and new, open to welcoming love into your life. Love is like chocolate. Some is hollow, some is bitter, much is sweet. We all taste the full array.

Pledging Oneself—A Rite of Dedication

Your search within the Craft has led you to this place of decision and commitment. You have set aside a space in your life for learning, intuition, and growth. Now it is time to formalize your intention to yourself, the elements, and the gods. Give thought to the length of time you can realistically vow to undertake. Traditionally, this is a year and a day; however, some studies or schools may run longer. You may wish to absorb the wisdom of a particular deity or a whole pantheon for a season or a full turn of the Wheel.

Plan ahead what you will say when you introduce yourself and state the reason for your quest. This part of the dedication is unscripted, as it is unique to each dedicant and situation. Remember, you are "one Witch" and this is your singular, hallowed, and holy way.

Withdraw now to a wild but safe place where you may work undisturbed. It is important for this pledging that you are in the heart of the Universe, among the elements that sustain and honor life.

On your altar, place a picture of yourself. Next, set there a symbol of the coursework, pantheon, or deity to which you will bind your energies. This can be as singular as a God or Goddess statue, or as universal as a picture of the deity you print from the Internet. If it's a course of study, write a few sentences describing it or place any welcome letter you've received from the teacher on your altar.

In wind-safe containers now position two candles: a white one and a yellow one. Lastly, bring gifts for the elements themselves. You may choose to hang a birdseed ball from a nearby tree for the beings of the air. Bottled water is advisable for any woodland jaunt, and a bit can be used to bless a nearby plant or shrub. You can bury a copper coin for fire, symbolizing a

fans the flames

thing of value, produced by heat and pressure. Trees treasure caresses and kind words in equal measure, but a tiny crystal is always welcome, too.

To summon the elements to come witness your rites, take with you a bell. It should be a melodic thing whose tone delights your ear when it rings.

Now it is time to begin. Slowly turn all around you, drinking in the beauty of the place. Imagine yourself as part of the nature that surrounds you. You might envision yourself as a sapling tree, roots planted in a grove of protective, sheltering, leafy elders. You might see yourself as the young stag with first velvet horns, prancing into this woodland glade, knowing that here you will find much to enrich and sustain you.

Use any imagery that calls to you and evokes your wild spirit within.

Turn to the east, doorway of new beginnings. Ring your bell and say:

> "Dawning of the day, I greet you! East is the home of vision and wisdom. I stand now at the threshold, embarking on that which is new. I come with a heart of hope. My spirit is filled with respect. In honor, this gift I bring. (*Hang the seed ball.*) Guide me on the journey ahead, winged ones, and blessed be."

Turn to the south, place of quickening. Ring your bell and say:

> "Light of noonday bright, I greet thee! South is the anvil and the forge, the place of transformation. I step forth now into the light, encouraged to take action. I come with a heart of courage. My spirit is fueled by commitment. In honor, this gift I bring. (*Bury your copper coin.*) Guide me

on the journey ahead, guardians of the fire, and
blessed be."

Turn to the west, place of emotional expression. Ring your bell
and say:

"Place of twilight and cooling shade, I greet thee!
West is the quenching drink, the mirrored pool
of reflection. I come now to ponder, to pore over
what I will learn. My heart will pose the questions; your spirit will murmur the answers. In
honor, this gift I bring. (*Pour out some of your bottled water.*) Guide me on the journey ahead, great
river of many streams, and blessed be."

Turn at last to the north, place of repose and nurturing. Ring
your bell and say:

"Place of midnight and deep repose, I greet thee!
North is the dream that brings knowledge, stories of the ancients now revealed. I come now
to sow the seeds of my growth that I might harvest enlightenment and truth. In honor, this gift I
bring. (*Go to the tree and stroke its bark, then bestow
your crystal.*) Guide me on the journey ahead, you
who have known many seasons, and blessed be."

Return to your altar and take up the photo of yourself. Hold
it in your hands, turning to each of the four elements. Imagine yourself shaking hands all around. Now introduce yourself,
just as you would at a gathering of honored guests who might
wish to know you better. This can be as informal as "Hi there,
I'm Sam Jacobson. This is a beautiful place, and I thank you for
sharing it with me. Let me tell you a bit about myself. Sometimes I feel the closeness of the gods when I'm out hiking in the
forest preserve, and I think they're trying to tell me something.

fans the flames

I've read some books and asked some questions and think I'm on the right path. Today, I'm pledging to make a space for the gods to talk to me and show me what might bring joy to me and make me a better person. Blessed be."

Place your photo back on the altar and take up the symbol of your spiritual commitment. If it is a course of study, describe it in your own words, just as you would enthusiastically tell a guest at a gathering about something that interested you. State the time frame this will take you to complete, and ask for the wisdom to pace yourself and stay true to your goal.

If you are pledging yourself to a god, goddess, or pantheon, address them directly.

Holding that representation in your hands, say something like:

> "Lady Rhiannon, I pledge to you that over the next six months, my apprenticeship in the healing arts be guided by your hand." Or: "Hail Tyr, Norse god of justice! Grant that in my term as a union steward for my company, I remember to seek fair resolutions in respect for all concerned."

Anything you say that comes from the earnest intent of your heart will not be wrong. The gods know good will and candor when they hear it.

Place the representation back on the altar. Then place your hand over your heart and say aloud:

> "This do I hereby vow, that I will keep an open mind and seek to know truth from illusion. I will embrace that which beckons me and partake of that which is for the ripening of my soul. I will speak my truth honorably and question that which is not to my highest good. I will stay

rooted in the pledge I have made on this day and pluck away any vines of doubt or disillusionment that may crop up in my weariness or frustration from time to time."

Thank any deities you have spoken to by name, and tell them you look forward to spending more quality time together. Starting with the north, thank the elements for joining you. End by saying, "May there be love and respect between us always. Farewell and blessed be." Kiss your fingertips in a farewell salute.

When all deities and powers have departed, take a few minutes to explore the place where your rite has been held. There may be a dedication gift for you, a token the gods have left in this place. See if a piece of bark on the ground catches your eye or a speckled feather waves to you as the breezes ripple the grass. A shiny stone may need to live in your pocket as a token of this day. You go your way, spirit rejoicing, steps eager to tread the path before you. It is done.

Strange Initiations . . . The Making of a Priestess

My priestess path has been a quizzical one, more like Harry Potter's dim Diagon Alley than Glenda's yellow brick road in the merry old Land of Oz. It started with a dream . . .

Having grown up in a haunted house, I'd developed a useful technique for pulling myself out of a dream into waking. I'd just simply say, as my dreaming self, "I choose not to dream this dream," and poof, it'd be gone and I'd be wide awake again. Not so with the dream that held me captive as an adult some fifteen years ago. I saw myself in profile, facing forward. A hammered silver disk on a chain (quicksilver, I was told in the dream) was being fastened by a pair of hands to hang around my neck. Okay, I was good with that; even my dreaming self knew that a necklace or medallion was a badge of honor, recognition for one's accomplishments. Cool.

But as the dream continued, the hands moved upward past my throat to clasp the chain behind my head, disk hanging on my brow. Oh no! I knew this drill, and what that meant, and what it was all about! The gods could just go pick on someone else! I yanked out my "get out of this dream free" card and tried to find the exit. No dice. As I stumbled out of bed, eyes open, and lurched into the living room, the dream was still dreaming me. No way would I be a priestess, I protested! I knew nothing about leading a group, being responsible for others' karmic connections, or joint works of magic. Not to mention having to do ritual in front of a crowd. My psyche was shaken, and I was quaking big time. One year later I was leading open circles and the road ran on from there.

I accepted an invitation to guest with a Mohsian coven. The idea of skyclad work set off some jitters with me. "I'm going to go be naked with a whole roomful of strangers!" I fretted and paced. My forever friend, Christian biker chick Joan, shook her head at me. "Did they tell you that you had to be nude?" she asked.

"Well . . . no . . . not exactly," I stammered in reply. "Then take a caftan," Joan suggested. "Wear it if you want and take if off if you feel comfortable later." Wow, why didn't I think of that? The big blue caftan that I wore to that first circle was so huge, I could've staked it at the corners and four of us could've gone camping in it. By gods, I would make those Witches work at it, if they had thoughts of peeling me!

Despite the joke about "ritual nudity sharpening eyesight," the tone was reverent. One by one, participants soaked in a candlelit meditation bath, then emerged into the ritual room nude. Focus was on the work to be done, and no one noticed a state of undress. I grew to love the other coven members and still think of them in my mind as my coven brothers and sisters. However, scripted ritual format was too confining for me. I studied for a turn of the Wheel, never sought initiation, and left the coven at Yule.

That Mohsian priestess did me a powerful boon though, when early on in my studies she insisted I choose a patron deity. One July evening I entered a fragranced tub, ringed by candlelight. Submerged up to my neck in lukewarm water, I closed my eyes and said aloud, "I do not know enough to choose any one of you . . . If someone wishes to work with me, please make your presence known."

Suddenly there were cool currents, like wind across the snow, swirling around my ankles and shoulders, both of which were underwater. My inward gaze filled with the image of a gray-bearded man in a billowing blue cloak, broad-brimmed hat dipped low over one eye. In one hand he held a walking staff. The other he extended to me, saying, "I come to you on the North Wind, and I will teach you."

I stammered, "Ulp! Yessir!" and went scrambling out of the tub! I frantically phoned a friend who had the *Witches' God* book by the Farrars. A sharp intake of breath on her end followed my description, then an "Oh no . . . I'm so sorry . . . that's Odin!" Okay, what was the terrible news I needed to know?

Turned out the old fellow was a trickster, a bit of a rake, a great sweet-talker with the ladies, and would go to any ends to gain wisdom or magic. Yes, he was the battle-father, the conniver, and the strategist. He was also the shaman who pierced himself to vision quest for the runes, and he was the wanderer who loved an unknown road, a boon companion, and stories to be heard around a stranger's fire. I took the hand he offered and have never been sorry. Odin is my teacher and my wayfar-

fans the flames

ing friend. When I had difficulty memorizing the runes, I cast a circle and went to the "source," asking for a clue and better retention. The runes speak to me now, and I see them everywhere.

The spring after leaving the coven I thought of the custom necklaces my former Mohsian priestess crafted for her initiates. What might mine have been like? I wistfully sighed. At a local rock and gem show, one lone strand of unpolished and chipped Baltic amber stole my gaze. As I paid the cost and hung it around my neck, I clairaudiently heard, "We gave it to you in time for Imbolc . . . enjoy." Had I been degreed by the hand of the gods?

If that was my first degree, my second was a doozy. Exactly one year later a phone call came from a very upset Wiccan fellow. His girlfriend, a onetime Satanist, was up to her old evil ways. He caught her invoking demons in the den and changed the locks posthaste. Now what to do about those nasty gates-of-hell vibes she'd thoughtlessly left behind? He wanted a house cleansing, a silver bullet, and some sage—not necessarily in that order.

I dialed up my former priestess, stammering out the wretched tale of what had been asked of me. One ought to be at least second or third degree to do work like that, I offered, trying to wiggle off the hook. Ha, she snorted! Either you knew this stuff or you didn't. Earn your field stripes, kid! She hung up and left me gaping at the phone.

I assembled a SWAT team and we blitzed the place. Some chanted and rang bells, others made a boundary of capsicum all around the place so that evil might be kept at bay. In the boudoir hung a portrait of the departed Princess of Darkness. Clad only in her cleavage and her crimson contact lenses, her gaze seemed to burn a hole right through my soul. I went trembling

fans the flames

to a mage who swiftly cleaned up that gnarly energy and neu-
tralized the place. As for the Princess of Darkness, she's now
belting out hymns and hallelujahs at the Liberty Street Gospel
Church's tent revival show. She's found familiar friends. Who
else but the devil herself has kept Christian churches in business all these years?

In later days I made the acquaintance of many magical special types. Ceremonial magicians and I tend to make each other
crazy. A lofty lord known as Boreus Supremus (we shall henceforth know him as "BS") was no exception. Because he lived in
a cramped studio apartment, BS liked to borrow my backyard
ritual space. One night, after performing his own private working, he left his complexly created astral temples all in place and
invited me to do any work of my own. I lit a single candle atop
the northern cairn, and bare-breasted except for amber, sang
runes and shrieked to the sky. BS shivered and wet himself!

I was therefore quite astonished when BS rang me up one
night and said he was on his way over. He had been led to
bestow upon me an ordination. Why? I asked. He said I would
know when the time was right.

BS roared into my driveway and dashed into the ritual
space with an armload of tiki torches, shoving them into the
ground. He lit them, then thrust at me a sword. Swear to the
Watchtowers, he ordered. Swear what? I asked. You guessed
it, I would know when the time was right. Impromptu oaths
done, BS dug a sterile lancet out of his pocket and squeezed
three drops of blood from my freshly pricked thumb. Yow,
that hurt! Why in the hell did he do that?! Yup, you know the
answer; say it with me, boys and girls. He daubed my blood on
a knotted chunk of rope, onto which was dripped red wax to
"seal my vow."

My Universal Life Church (ULC) credentials would arrive in the mail soon, he said, and so they did. I buried the rope in the desert, not wanting the cops to stop me for a tail light and suspect me of darker deeds. In keeping with his secretive tradition, BS never mentioned the ULC website or disclosed that I could have signed up online and dispensed with the theatrics. Why? Guess I'll know when the time is right.

Sea Mother Spell to Bring Love Your Way

You will need for this working: two seashell-shaped candle holders or large seashells themselves; two votive candles in ocean colors such as soft blue, aquamarine, or mauve; sea salt, rose oil, and rose incense; aura-cleansing bath salts; and a tumbled sea stone, for polishing the rough edges in you. A river rock, smoothed by water, will also suffice. The waters of the world are one. You may wish to play an instrumental or ocean sounds CD as background for your meditation, and you will need some time alone for inner reflection.

This three-part spell will take several moon phases to bring results and will require effort on your part—not just quick results. Be therefore earnest in your longing to bring love your way.

Phase I: The opening
To be repeated for seven Friday nights . . .
On a Friday night, sacred to Venus and begun under new moon, fill your tub with warm, fragrant waters. You may wish to add a few drops of rose oil for loving, and/or a few grains of aura-cleansing bath salts, whatever calls to you. Set up your seashell candle altar some safe place nearby, where it can be seen. Keep the sea salt and ocean stone within reach of the tub. Light the candles, saying:

"I summon the love and wisdom of the great Sea
Mother. I seek to love and be loved in return, and I
ask that love come to me on the tide. I enter your
womb, that answers might be murmured and
heard, and that I might emerge smooth and joyous once again. Lady, please come. Let your touch
be felt and your voice be heard. Blessed be."

Take some of the sea salt and scatter it into your bath water,
drawing an invoking pentagram and saying as you do:

"As salt purifies and renews, let those places in me
that are hard, angry, or resistant become softened
and shining once again. Dissolve my despair and
leave love glistening in its place. So mote it be."

Enter the bath and soak by candlelight. Close your eyes and
reflect on the barriers you have erected to keep love out—e.g.,
old baggage, feelings of low self-worth, preconceived notions,
and so forth. Envision those things as hard grainy crystals,
slowly worn away and dissolved by the salt water and carried
off on the tide to a place you cannot see. See yourself in your
mind's eye as a new, receptive, gentler being. You hold out your
hand in this meditation, and someone's hand is there to take
it. There is such joy in finding the other half of you! Savor this
sensation and the knowledge that there does exist for you in
this world a perfect partner.

Say to the Goddess, "I know there is work to be done
before I receive this blessing. Therefore, tumble me smooth
upon your waves, make me a thing of love and delight, a vessel
of giving and receiving. I yield to your loving embrace."

Take the ocean stone now and work your way over chakra
points, pausing at each to reflect upon, silently or aloud, what
blockages might have kept you from loving wholly in the past.

fans the flames

For instance, were you too busy with mundane dross to honor the lover in someone else or to remember to be the lover yourself? Did your intuition perhaps lead you in someone's direction, but your reason veered you away? Was there love you never expressed? As you run the smooth stone over your body, honor the lessons of those times of missed opportunity but know that there is healing and openness taking place.

Conclude your bath and meditation when you are ready, telling the Sea Mother that you will make her a gift of your love and yourself. Thank her for attending you and state that you know that when you have finished the needed self-work and are ready, your lover will come.

Phase II: Making your promise real

Do some small thing to improve yourself and put yourself in the path of others. Take a walk, join a nice witchy book club, take an inexpensive self-improvement or special interest class where other interesting souls will likely show up, too. Open up and share little bits of yourself. Remember the good and engaging things about others. This phase is ongoing.

Phase III: The summoning

When seven Fridays have passed since first you began your spell, revisit your Sea Mother altar and fragrant bath but with a different focus in mind. Invoke the Sea Mother and state:

> "Great Sea Mother, whose hands hold all mysteries and whose treasures are revealed with the tide, I am ready for that jewel I seek. Send to me now my own true love, and let me know that one, when he/she is placed before me. Let there be recognition, connection, honor, and respect between us."

(List any other specifics you may have for your perfect partner as well . . . e.g., unattached, of common spiritual background, whatever is most important to you.)

Then address the lover who is waiting to meet you:

"Beloved, I have waited a long time for you. My arms have been empty and my life has been incomplete. I have made a space for you and will cherish you as the gift you are. I welcome you into my life and my heart, and will know you when you stand before me. I bid you hasten into my life, that we may be together and fully love one another."

Blow a kiss across the cosmic tide to the one who is on the way. Thank the Sea Mother for her aid in bringing the thing about. Keep your eyes, heart, and spirit open. One never knows the direction from which love may come.

One Golden Rose

Is there one you have noticed passing by? One who turns your head and whose musical laughter haunts your days? Do you wonder how to open conversation, to draw closer and see if magic happens? Here is what one Witch might do.

Begin this work at new moon, the time of bringing good things into new beginnings. You will need a gold-colored candle, a royal blue candle, and a tightly furled yellow rose. Have the florist wrap up one that's still so snug it's almost a bud, for it will serve you well. You may also wish to have pleasant incense and unobtrusive instrumental music.

Set aside some quiet time and fresh-snip the stem of your yellow rose, placing it in a vase with water. Say out loud, "I offer this rose to [person's name] in honor and in friendship, that if it is our mutual wish, [name] and I might begin to talk more and become better acquainted. This rose is my invitation

fans the flames

to [name] to get to know me, that we might discover common ground." By phrasing it this way, you are expressing a wish but respecting the free will you both possess.

Next, light the royal blue candle, saying, "May the words exchanged between [name] and me be of the highest integrity. May there be earnest regard and truth between us always." When conversation between you begins, you both need to state what you are truly thinking and feeling. What good would dialogue be if you both were merely out to impress and not being your real selves?

Lastly, light the gold-colored candle, saying, "In all ways, [name], I will accept you and whatever you share with me. I will honor our mutual will. If we cease being strangers and become abiding friends, you will always have my best intentions, my sincerity, and my discretion. [Name], I wish for you all things shining and blessed, that are for your highest good."

Light your candles awhile each night, until they are burned up and gone. Allow the rose to open, and savor every bit of beauty each loosening petal reveals. Do not be surprised if the Goddess in her nimble manner opens your heart as well.

The North Star Descends

Here is the tale of my voyage upon the sea of love. It's a saga of searching and of finding, in the last place I'd ever look, the one who guards my heart and guides my dreams.

It started with a dream, in my Illinois bell tower. One morning I awoke, tears on my cheeks and an ache in my heart for the lover who waited somewhere, though his face wasn't clear to me. In the dream, my daughter Ang had found me doing dishes, arms deep in soapsuds at the kitchen sink.

"Mom, someone's waiting for you," she told me.

"You'll have to bring them here," I scowled. "Can't you see I'm busy?"

She shook her head. "No, Mom, you have to go to them." I dried my hands on my dishtowel and, grumbling, went along.

We arrived at the base of a tall dark hill, where a man called down to me, "Bronwynn! Come see what I've brought you!" He seemed excited and eager to see me. I climbed to the top of the hill and discovered that he had brought seeds and bags of rich, sweet-smelling earth. We dug the holes and planted together, hands dirty, heads bumping as we companionably worked together. I had a vague recognition of his face and a sense of easy familiarity but didn't know where to find him in the world.

I knew that planting a garden is a metaphor for putting down roots, building a life. To entrust someone else with your garden is a powerful, vulnerable thing. To discover that your garden mirrors another's is a marriage of the soul.

Perhaps my love awaited in the Pacific Northwest, home of my heart, I thought. When I came to dwell there, I scanned the faces of strangers, found no soulmate there. Along the sandy stretches of Larrabee State Park I created the rune Gebo for partnership out of pinecones, and placed them in the shallows, sending my message of longing on the tide. With magical family up in Birch Bay, I brewed up herbs in an old crab pot hung over a driftwood fire. We ran, carrying our makeshift cauldron, to fling the elixir to the waves, crying, "To the sea! To the sea!" Although I formed great friendships and made unforgettable memories, my heart mate wasn't there.

I stayed in touch with friends in Arizona but never let on to Rowan, Storm, or Dan that work was scarce in Bellingham and my last weeks there were spent living in my van. I scrubbed up with bottled water and a cake of lavender soap, donned work clothes in the woods, and hoped like hell I hadn't hung my undies on a poison ivy vine. Ultimately, I returned to

Phoenix, closer to family and more plentiful employment, and re-immersed myself in the Pagan community here. Although I was surrounded, I was very much alone. I feared that my love and I had missed connections, up north by the water's edge.

Then one July night in 2003 things began to shake. As I browsed eBay for witchy T-shirts from Salem, Massachusetts, a china pattern from sellers there called North Star kept popping up. North Star, North Star, innumerable pages that night.

In August I attended a message service at a small spiritualist fellowship in Phoenix. When I adjourned to the healing room for an energy massage, the gods spoke. The Reiki master stopped abruptly and came around front to face me. She took my hands, an incredulous look on her face, and said:

"This means nothing to me, but they say it means something to you. The North Star is not where you think it is." She leaned her head as though listening, then grinned. "Buckle up," she said. "They're telling me it will be quite a ride!"

My jaw dropped, as the lines of that poem I had written some twenty-five years ago went flashing through my mind. I'd penned them for someone in the distance, my North Star, whom I had one day longed to find.

In the early part of September I flew to California and attended a Goddess festival. Among the workshop offerings was one on Norse seidth magic, an ancient oracular tradition. The veiled seeress sat on a lofty perch, an intricately carved wooden chair so high that her feet could not touch the ground. She was literally suspended between the worlds. Trance songs and hallowing songs were sung, then festival querents approached and posed their questions.

When my turn came I was deliberately vague. "When shall the North Star descend?" I wanted to know.

The oracle pondered, then answered cryptically, "You must magnetize a stone. Then shall the North Star descend." I thought she meant a lode stone with magnetic sand. That has never appealed much to me, but politely I said I would keep that in mind.

In September our third annual Phoenix Pagan Pride Day drew nigh, with trials and triumphs galore. A few days before the event, my stregan friend Michele and I went to a mountain preserve. We cast white carnations into a fire and asked blessings on folk who deserved them, and who we felt needed them most.

Among the nominees was our dear friend Dan, who had put his shoulder to wheel, pouring energy, effort and resources into keeping the Pagan Pride Day alive. Michele and I had been his stalwart supporters, and sometimes his tormenters as well. She and I extolled Dan's virtues and voiced aloud that he needed a partner in the Pagan community. This ought to be a woman with her own identity in the magical community. This wonderful gal should be independent, resourceful, and should cherish Dan for the jewel he was.

As we departed our circle, Michele stopped by the standing stone at one end of the ramada, a bemused look on her face. "Bronwynn, who is Freya?" she asked. I answered, "Goddess of love, witchcraft, and war. Why?"

Michele laid our last white carnations as offerings on the stone. We wedged a smoldering charcoal block into a crevice in the rock and tossed on intoxicating white musk incense. Then, like happy-hearted children, the strega and I joined hands and skipped around the rock, singing, "We love you, Freya! We promise to always be open to love!" We threw our arms in the air and giggled like giddy nymphs. We had just unwittingly magnetized a stone.

A few days later, a dear mage friend named Roderick lay dying in an East Valley nursing home. In my tiny apartment I lit a candle and held vigil, waiting for the call from his friends that I knew would sadly come. I thanked Roderick for his kindness, laughter, and the stories I still retell. Sensing myself not alone, I asked if there was energy in the room. One panel of my vertical blinds detached from the rest, and began rocking to and fro. I was nudged to go break out my Norse Tarot and lay out a reading for myself. A strange time to do that, but I complied. I remembered all the times Roderick had cast and read runes for me, sometimes behind the wheel of his car, ripping down the interstate in full trance. I never questioned then; why should I doubt now?

My card, the Queen of Swords, fell first. Then next to it, for the first time ever, came her counterpart, the King. The Queen cleaves away swiftly and cleanly what must pass; the King surveys the long-range battlefield and maps his strategy. Perfectly paired. A third card showed the "giving": a man stood behind his wife, bestowing on her a necklace garnered in his trade. The sharing of material goods and emotional ones as well. I blew out my candle and went to bed, not knowing what to think.

The following night came a knock on my door. Dan, aware that Roderick had been taken off life support, knew that the wizard was waning. Dan brought a bottle of mead, to honor our memories of Roderick and to talk. We spoke of many things, of roads we both had traveled, of honor and of our longing to be loved. We examined our obligations—mine to the gods, his to a marriage long grown cold. Friends talked into the night, and we discovered we were more.

On the morning of October's Pagan Pride Day, running on shreds of sleep, Michele and I arrived at the park. I wore an autumn garland atop my crispy head. We found Dan seated, surveying the vendors setting up.

"Doesn't Bronwynn look pretty?" Michelle chirped. Dan agreed I did, and he looked up. I fell headlong into his eyes, my denim jeans replaced by a mental image of myself in rough-spun, a lifetime ago in Denmark. I watched myself sink down on one knee, laying my cheek on his hand, and I heard myself whisper the words, "Will you have me, m'lord?"

In January 2006 we were wed by the hand of Lady Kate. We limboed under the broom, to the strains of Led Zeppelin's "Immigrant Song." We cut a pentacle-shaped cake and drank punch from the bubbling cauldron my grandkids stirred. We toasted to one another beside that standing stone. As Dan said to me one late night riding home, holding hands in the car, "I can't tell where I leave off and you begin."

I have pulled into port and dropped anchor. Every wave is sparkling bright. My heart is finally home.

On Loving

Carry your roots in your pocket,
Though loved ones be not at your side.
Friendships can never be altered
If deep in your heart they abide.

fans the flames

December

January

February

March
the winds of change

April

May

June

July

August

September

October

November

Pegasus

Who dares to bridle Pegasus
And sail the great Beyond
Borne on the wings of memory,
Elusive as a song?
Outside the senses lies a realm
Where dreams alone exist;
Come closer, share the Mystery
Peer deeper through the mist.
The human soul has sonar wings
To skim across the tide.
Will you dare to ride,
Laying fear aside,
Wild Pegasus in his flight . . . ?

The word on the wind is *change*. All of us attuned can feel subtle stirrings this time of year. "The wind is shifting," we say, or we repeat the Irish blessing, "May the wind be ever at your back." Winds can freshen or flatten, are worthy of our invoking and our respect. The rituals contained in this chapter are designed to clear the air, and to bring in the energy of breezy spring.

Sometimes life gets battered and backlashed, and hearts wind up in a tangle. In this chapter you will find a ritual to calm the storm that rages between you and another, that peace may be restored. A good gust of wind can separate, blowing all that is strong one direction and all that is groundless in another. I offer you a sorting ritual, to choose which burdens are rightfully your own and which to let fall behind. Lastly in this blustery chapter you will find a celebration, a full-blown (pun intended) wind ritual. Enjoy!

Skadi, Goddess of the Snows

How beautiful, I thought! I lay in meditation one spring night, eyes closed but watching as a diamond dust column of snow spun in the frosty air. I thought of the tulips and hyacinths pushing their way through the snow of my Illinois garden a week before Ostara. I had cursed the last soft snow, wishing it away from the waking earth underneath. Winter had taken its financial toll with high heating bills and car repairs. Winter was cruel, I thought. Now here was a vision of snow. What could the message be?

As I watched entranced, the snow began to dance. Shimmers swirled as flakes took on form on the frostfields and reveled in the ecstasy of life, of untamed freedom. Then she was there, dark eyed, cloaked in white fur with a polar bear at her side. Her eyes met mine, telling me to pay heed. From a pouch, the goddess took a hook of bone and cast out over the ice. It sliced through with ease, sank deep. The polar bear lumbered after and soon came back with fish.

Again she sought my eyes, stared at me intently. Did I get it? Did I understand? Suddenly I did. I had the "hook," the means of providing for myself and those I loved. Skadi had shown me the needed tool, already within my grasp. I took notice and came back into awareness.

The message of Skadi is, "Pick up your own bow and carry it." She's not one to coddle, but she will walk the snowfields beside you. Many has been the northern morning when the Huntress walked beside me over the silvered grass. The icicle is her spear, the snowy sky her domain. She taught me that all is beauty, and that to "winter" is to watch for the abundance that will come despite the lingering snows. Hail the Winter Queen, as she tarries into spring.

Calming the Storm

The March winds are stirring and tugging at our heartstrings. There is no perfect reconciliation time, especially where there may have been angry words followed by sullen silences between family and friends. Here is a communication spell for healing a hurt between you and someone you love. I have entitled this ritual "Calming the Storm" because that is where the work begins—with the time of hurt being viewed as leading to an impending storm. The results the spell strives to bring about are the healing of old heart wounds, which will unblock the free flow of communication, thus ultimately ending at least in neutrality and hopefully a more harmonious relationship down the line.

Please note that this spellwork is not manipulative in nature. You are seeking to bring about renewed communication; you are not attempting to control the estranged person's actions or responses.

Here is what you will need:

- 1 "stormy" blue-purple taper candle . . . a color that hits you as brooding or overcast
- 1 light sky-blue candle . . . the shade the sky turns after a good rousing thunderstorm
- 1 rose quartz-colored pink candle . . . to send happiness and health to the one with whom you've had words
- Anointing oil . . . while I prefer Eye of the Cat's "Harmony Oil" for this working, any blessing oil that you select will do

In new moon phase, anoint the storm-sky candle, projecting into it all of your sadness and regret about the falling out. Note: you are not assuming guilt or blaming the distanced party for the rift, but simply acknowledging how sorry you are that it occurred in the first place and divided the two of you.

Inscribe your name or initials and those of the other party, adding a suitable word like *peace, harmony,* or *friendship*. Invoke the aspect of Deity you deem most appropriate to carry out your message on the astral plane. Let this candle burn completely out.

During a turbulent time with my teenage daughter, very much a warrior maid, I asked Artemis to send to her my blessings and my love. Unlikely deities may step forward and offer their assistance, as one did for me during a time of family strife. During a meditation, my mind's eye was filled with billowing, wind-swept foam. A voice from the waves said softly, "I am Oceanus, father of the waters that encircle the world. I will calm the storm." I looked him up, found he was legit, and gratefully accepted his unsolicited aid.

Wait three days, then contact the person with whom you are at odds. What you hear at this point may not be particularly pleasant, but exercise restraint. Be patient, be calm. This is the storm finally breaking. Tell them they are sorely missed, then go.

The day after this communication has occurred, take up the pale blue candle. Anoint and invoke as before, but this time ask for a peaceful resolution between you and the one you love. Again, allow the candle to burn completely out.

Wait three more days, then make contact again. This time you may still receive some reproachful comments, but things should be quieter and feel more solid. At this point it is far more important for you to listen than to speak. Tell the person honestly how much regard you have for them, then leave.

On the following day, burn the rose-quartz candle, anointing and invoking once again. Envision sweet spring breezes and the merest scent of blossoms on the wind. Send this sense of freshness and renewal to your loved one, extending your hope of restored closeness into the candle flame. Imagine the kindest of words, or perhaps shared laughter, flowing between you once again. Close your working with a psychic hug and let the candle burn itself completely out.

While I realize this spell takes nearly two weeks to complete, the mending it can bring about is infinitely worth it. When old hurts have become insignificant, the healing work is done. A white rose on your altar, in thanks to the gods, is enough.

Johnny's Box—A Rustle in the Leaves

It had taken me years to track down a photo of my Cherokee Grandpa Johnny, but there it was in my hands. I gazed at his eyes and discovered my own, dark with elongated creases at the corners, in a high-cheekboned face. John Samuel, my paternal grandfather, one quarter Cherokee. Even at sixty-five, the age he was when this retirement photo was taken, Johnny's hair was still crow's feather black. He and I had had an unspoken connection all my life and a large part of his.

Johnny was a believer. He ordered a spook out of his bedroom one night because it was too damned late to come calling! As a child I would perch on his lap and he'd read *FATE* magazine ghost stories aloud to me. No sugarplum tales for me, but rather the headless haunt of such-and-such a place.

When Johnny died of a heart attack at age seventy-eight, I didn't plan on driving the hundreds of miles to his funeral. I worked long hours and was the young mother of two infants. The budget for gas was bare, and I planned to pay my respects right where I was.

All that changed the afternoon that Grandpa Johnny invited me down. As I propped up my weary feet, after hearing the news of his death, I began to doze. Dreaming, I watched myself walk up his driveway, saw his hound dog drowsing by

the winds of change

the well. My feet carried me on around the back of the house where Johnny sat napping in a wicker rocking chair, straw hat shading his brow. As I approached, he opened his eyes and said sadly to me, "Won't you come see me just one more time . . . ?" I made the drive down.

At his funeral I closed my eyes for the benediction. Suddenly my mind's eye was filled with the image of a white dove, winging over the old railroad yard where Johnny had worked most of his life. It circled around the boxcars, hovered for a moment, then was gone. Johnny had flown home.

Through the decades I remembered him fondly. Then two years ago, there came a rustle in the leaves and Johnny had a message for me. I was walking to my apartment laundry room when I had the strongest urge to sit my basket down and wrap my arms around the pine tree nearest to me. No one was around, so I laid my cheek against the tree's bark as well. All at once, Johnny was everywhere. There was a gift for me, he said, and wrapped me in a hug. A wandering breeze blew through the branches, his goodbye for now.

What a treasure trove came my way soon after! Johnny's widowed daughter-in-law, tidying up the attic, came upon a cardboard box. She opened it and saw the sheaf of cowboy short stories typed on brittle onion skin inside. She told me that I was the first grandchild that came to mind, and she headed for the post office that same day.

As I carefully place each near-transparent page in my leather-bound photo album, I feel Johnny's hand on mine. I note the penciled word count below his return address and know that Grandpa hoped one day to see his works in print. To my knowledge he never did, but because of Johnny's love of words, I cherish them as well. Up through his line, this book has come to be.

the winds of change

Outside, just now, my wind chimes softly chinkled and the aspens waved hello. Johnny is passing by.

Sorting It Out with Sticks

Sometimes it seems that all the world's a burden. Everywhere you turn, you find confusion, strife, uncertainty, and guilt. Issues mount into a bundle, and it's time to sort it out.

Take with you the following things: a small piece of burlap or other rough fabric, and a piece of twine to tie it with. Also obtain a piece of soft leather, red ribbon with which to tie it, any beads you may want to affix to the ribbon, and a feather to tuck into it. Take a pinch of tobacco to burn for the Grandfathers, and a little pouch of cornmeal to leave for the spirits of the place. Set out into the nearest woods or wild place, and gather up sticks as you walk. You will need at least a dozen of them, more if they call to you and readily come to hand.

Light the tobacco, either using a small shell to smolder it in or lighting a small mound of it atop a rock. Close your eyes and turn slowly to the four directions, saying:

> "Grandfathers of the east, grant vision here. May it be that I see with eagles' eyes what is hidden from my present sight. Aho!
>
> Grandfathers of the south, grant courage here. May it be that I have the strength of heart to take the action needed. Aho!
>
> Grandfathers of the west, grant release here. May it be that my hand can let go as well as hold fast. Aho!
>
> Grandfathers of the north, grant knowledge here. May my tongue know the words to speak, to untangle, to lay clear. Aho!"

Bundle the sticks and roll the burlap around them, tying them loosely. Sit yourself comfortably on the ground. Take a moment to center yourself and clear your spirit, then consider the first complication before you. Name it aloud, saying:

"Here is the issue of _____ . Wisdom of the forest,
what is it that I should know?"

Reach your hand toward the bundle of sticks, pulling out the one that your fingers seem drawn to. Run your fingers along the length of the stick as you think on the situation. If the twig curves and veers in its configuration, you may encounter evasiveness or reluctance on the other person's behalf, as you attempt to sort the matter out. If there are knots or burls on the twig, you may need to know that you will hear—and have to face—some harsh truths, as you attempt to bring this issue to a close. If the ends of the stick are splintered, the connection between you and the other person may have begun to unravel a long time ago, and perhaps this current conflict is heralding the "last straw." Is there a fork in the branch? If so, perhaps after speaking together and sifting through the matter, a time of apartness is best. Allow for the chance that a healing space may mend things between you again.

Ask the spirit of the wood, "Is this burden truly mine?" Oftentimes we take on baggage that is not our own, out of sympathy or a sense of obligation. We feel strongly that someone we loved has been wronged, and we are drawn into the battle. Can we be in loving, staunch support and still conserve our own energies without being drained by choosing up sides?

As you sort through your burdens, make three piles. Those issues to which you arrive at a clear resolution, and your mind perceives a well-defined plan of action, lay in the first. Those will become an offering to a small spirit fire you will build, returning them to the Grandfathers and thanking them for their aid. At the end of your sorting, gather these up for the fire, saying, "For these trials and the peace beyond them, do I give thanks. Aho."

For those burdens not rightfully yours, at the end of those contemplations, break the stick in half. At the end of those sortings, you will pick up those pieces and fling them out into the forest, saying, "I rejoice in the freedom of release. My burden is lighter, my steps are stronger, and my heart can breathe again. Aho."

If there are issues about which you still cannot, at this time, come to a conclusion, and will need to mull over further and carry awhile longer, place those in a third pile. At the end of your sortings, wrap these reverently in the soft leather and ribbon, saying, "These burdens are rightfully mine and shall resolve in their season." Tuck in the feather, adding, "May they sit lightly on my heart and spirit until they can be released in love and joy. Aho."

Kindle your spirit fire and thank the Grandfathers for their counsel and their blessing. Scatter the cornmeal on the ground, saying as you depart, "Blessings to the Old Ones of this place. There is wisdom here, and peace. I leave behind my token of gratitude."

Walk on, with clarity of thought, lightness of heart, and a much smaller bundle of burdens.

Winds of Spring Ritual

Pinwheels have been tied to the sides of the ramada, both for decoration and for later use in ritual by those who wish to use them. A central spring-themed altar sits at center circle. People enter, singing any "windy" chant that pleases you and that you can easily teach.

After all have been anointed and welcomed, the singing ends and quarters are invoked.

East: "Direction of the dawning day, breath of spring, scent of blossoms. Welcome now and blessed be."

South: "Warmth of noonday bright, earth awakener, dream stirrer. Welcome now and blessed be."

West: "Inertia melting, life reforming, liquid crystal longings. Welcome now and blessed be."

North: "Bones of life itself, ever resurrected. Majesty of mountains, welcome now and blessed be."

High Priestess (HPS) says: "In time so long forgotten that the stars were mere twinkles in Jupiter's eye and the seas a mighty mist, a goddess dwelt who held the night and day equally in her hands. Daybright and Firebright were the steeds who pulled her chariot across the morning sky. Beautiful Eos she was called, Goddess of the Dawn, sister to Selene the moon and Helios the sun."

Eos, stepping forth: "I am she who brings light to all the mortals of this earth and to the immortal gods who rule the wide sky. With rosy fingers, I paint new hope where once was uncertainty. At dawn all things are possible, as day springs forth anew. Listen to the singing of the morning lark, look to the morning star still brilliant in the sky.

Whisper your dreams on the wind, and they will reach my ears. I will rock them in my arms as the silver moon sinks low and wrap them in rainbow hues as the golden sun leaps forth from behind the clouds. I am a lover of many things, and hearts have quickened with the dawn. The Four Winds are the children of my longings . . ."

Boreas (North Wind), stepping forth: "I am Boreas, North Wind, haste maker, dream shaker. I encourage expediency, that the harvest is swiftly gathered. My touch is seldom gentle, and only the strongest of what is grown will stand. When you hear me come howling 'round your door, latch the shutters tight. Be sure that your grain bin is filled and your comforters are warm. I will try the strength of any situation, your resourcefulness and endurance. Yet I aid those with courage. If it is transformation you seek, the North Wind has carved peaks and hollowed valleys. Mine is the power of Change."

Eurus (East Wind), stepping forth: "I am Eurus, warm wind from the east, giver of sweet spring rains. My touch is gentle, and I hear the whispers of poets, seekers, and lovers. Raindrops, dewdrops, teardrops . . . they are much alike and I honor them all.

My warm breath is welcome relief from the North Wind's icy blast. I encourage green things to come forth, hearts and minds to open everywhere. If there is hope that you hold against your breast, words you yearn to speak, ears you would have hear your words, let me be your aid. I am Possibility."

Notus (South Wind), stepping forth: "I am Notus, the autumn gale, unexpected frenzy of the foamy seas. Do not seek to avoid all confrontation, as the air must be cleared. My billowing fog is as inevitable as the times you cannot see clearly, and bang against the reef. The way is sometimes obscured and your senses may mislead, but I will part the mist and guide you through. Have you the heart to ask for resolution? Are you ready for the answers that will stand revealed when the storms and trials of life abate? Know that there are rocks along the way and currents swift as thought itself. If you would see an end to struggle and to strife, call on me. I am the journey of Justice."

Zephyrus (West Wind), stepping forth: "I am Zephyrus, the light caress. In contrast to my brother's heavy hand (*looks pointedly at the North Wind*), I delight in the rustle of grasses and the fragrance of orchards. Many a lover has felt my fingers in their hair, my breath against their cheek. Many a lace has come undone, many a shutter has opened to my touch. Lovers murmur and lie entwined, summer nights are sweet as honeysuckle on the vine. If you would ease your spirits and leave care and caution behind, I am here.

Open your heart and your hands and turn your face to me. I am the kiss of Joy."

Eos: "Let your wishes, silent and spoken, be borne upon the Winds. Lighter than air, carried easily into the heavens, to the realm of the gods."

Chant: "Blowing winds, surging strong,
Restless ones of air;
Send our dreams where they belong;
O Winds, take us there!"

The cone of power builds and people blow on the pinwheels until the blades are gaily spinning. Ground and center by taking three deep breaths and sighing them out loudly: "Aaaaah!"

High Priest (HP), releasing quarters: "Powers of earth, air, fire, and water . . . blessings and thanks from your sons and daughters. As you depart to your own fair realms, our love goes ever with you. Blessed be."

HPS, releasing Deity: "Beautiful Eos, may we glimpse your face each rosy dawn, and remember your love for us. Stay if you will, go if you must, and blessed be."

HP: "This rite is ended; may the Winds of spring blow gently. Blessed be."

Wind Working

Blow east and west and south and north!
O, blow the answers I seek forth!
Blow them on the morning breeze,
Let me understand with ease
The words on the wind today.

January

February

March

April
the child in us all

May

June

July

August

September

October

November

December

Two Little Girl Frogs

Two little girl frogs went to town,
Each one dressed in a satin gown.
Golden slippers for each to wear,
And a crown of diamonds in their hair.
Two little boy frogs, a handsome sight.
One in black and the other in white
Said, "Pretty maids, may we dance with you
And maybe sing a song or two?"
Four little frogs, merry as could be
Danced in the shade of a big oak tree.
Laughing, singing, feeling fine,
They dined on honey and apple wine.
Then they noticed it was getting late,
So they all ran home at half-past eight.

This chapter, dedicated to the month of spring's unfolding, celebrates the young ones coming up in our midst. Whether children of our blood or the offspring of our hearts, kids rediscover the world for us. In the face of a child we see the mirror of our own soul—hopeful, trusting, open. To a child, all things are possible.

As new life prepares to enter this world, we can sing it safely through.

Suggested workings are rites to honor transitions into young manhood and young womanhood.

Finally, you will find a fun, downright silly children's circle that the kids can present at a grown-up gathering. Have fun, dear readers, and don't forget to play!

Andromeda's Lullaby

Each pregnancy is unique, and so should be the blessing for each child safely born. My daughter Angela easily became pregnant with my grandson Arthur, now eight. Her hair and body glowed; she worked out several times a week, never felt better in her life. When Andromeda (Andi) came along three years later, nature changed its tune. Weeks of trying for another child went by. When Ang finally did become pregnant, she felt drained and tired, caught colds easily, and wearily rode out the last months of the pregnancy.

I visited them in Maine, soon after Arthur was born, while dad Kevin was on a submarine out at sea. Arthur's blessing came about one autumn afternoon, as I watched him. I carried him to the patio, where a small grove of potted trees stood. "Grant this child health and endurance," I prayed aloud. "Let him honor his roots but never be afraid to reach up high for what he desires." I looked in the distance at the wooded marsh beyond. "May the waters of the world grant that he knows no limitations on what he may achieve. May love and self-confidence flow into his life." I looked up at the sky and said simply, "May the air allow his mind to always be open and respectful to the ways of those who are different, but may he know where his safety lies." I carried Arthur inside and glanced at Angela's fragranced candle burning. "May he have the spark of imagination," I wished for him, "and a will of his own to make his dreams come true." Arthur has eager curiosity, academic brilliance, and is rapidly learning social skills.

With Andi more intervention was required, even before she was born. Doctors were worried, no heartbeat could be found. I lit a white candle and called to my granddaughter's spirit by the name her mother had chosen for her while still a child herself. "Andi," I said, "we're waiting for you. You need to wrap up whatever you're doing and come join us now." I had a mental image of an older child, a tall honey-blonde girl, surrounded by other children and adults. She cocked her head for a second, as if listening, then the scene was gone. I sang her a lullaby I had written, just for calling her. You may wish to write a summoning song yourself, to call a babe to you. Every child deserves a lullaby. It doesn't matter if you sing like a wounded moose. Babies hear only the love and not whether you can carry a tune. Make up whatever melody comes to mind. My words went something like this:

> "Tiny sprite, spark of life
> We have gathered to greet you.
> Shining bright on this night
> We are eager to meet you.
> Come to the home that is safe and warm,
> Let the Lady guide you.
> All your days, all your ways,
> We'll stand loving beside you."

I pinched out my candle and smiled. Two weeks later tests came back positive, and Andi was on her way. Later in the pregnancy, however, doctors were concerned. Not only were the sonograms gender-inconclusive, the baby being coy, but now they couldn't find a heartbeat at all.

Once again I sang to her. The words were different this time, reaffirming our love for her and sending her strength to make the passage through. A few days later the ultrasound revealed a healthy Andi, who threw her arms up over her head in utero, spread her legs, and did a shimmy dance! No doubt about it, she'd make her entrance soon. Feisty and determined, Andromeda goes singing through the day. Is it any wonder, when that was the first thing she ever heard?

Boy's Rite of Passage into Manhood

Adorn your altar with pinecones, seasonal flowers, and symbols of the fertile earth. A God/Goddess candle and a protection jar candle should also be in place. Choose colors that evoke those energies for you. Quarter gifts, symbolic elemental blessings to be bestowed upon the young man, may also be placed on the altar for charging.

> **Air:** Jar of appropriate incense, Forest Lord of another resin blend
>
> **Fire:** New blade or athame
>
> **Water:** Clear bowl of spring water
>
> **Earth:** Pouch of seeds

Patio torches stand lit at each quadrant. This rite is best done at sundown, as it signals the ending of one phase of life—boyhood—in preparation for the next.

Before the ritual begins, the boy should undergo a meditation bath. Essential herbs and oils deemed appropriate are added to the water. This is a candlelit bath, as unhurried as he wishes, for the sole purpose of reflecting upon the solemnity and honor of this occasion and the growth he has known thus far. If possible, the boy's father and mother (or other adults he is close to, in a parental capacity) should serve as HP and HPS for this rite. Those invoking elemental quarters should all be male, relatives or friends older than the boy. The ritual space will have been smudged and swept before, and cleansed of all negativity. Circle may be cast before or after the boy's entrance into the sacred space, depending on your tradition. Attendees should bring drums and rattles, to raise energy later in the rite.

> **HPS:** "How do you enter this circle?"
>
> **Boy:** "I come in perfect peace and perfect love."

HP: "For what purpose do you enter?"

Boy: "To claim my rite of passage into manhood."

HPS: "We bid you welcome, _____ [*boy's given or magical name, according to his preference*]."

HP: "Heed me well, my son. Listen, learn, and live well. A man can do no greater thing than to live his life by these precepts."

At this point, the boy is welcomed into circle, anointed and embraced. The boy then goes to stand before the altar, everyone gathering around him. HP and HPS stand opposite the boy.

HPS: "Let it be known to all that we are gathered here for the sacred purpose of honoring _____ 's journey into manhood."

HP: "My son, this night you begin your transition into manhood. This is a spiritual as well as a physical transformation, which must not be taken lightly. It is your right to choose which path you will walk. As you consider, remember our Rede: 'And it harm none, do what you will.' I implore you to live by this ideal."

HPS: "Many are the responsibilities that accompany this new phase of life. Bear in mind that the measure of a man is not only his deeds but the quality of his life. Live your life with a gentle strength, for it is the strong man who needs not fight. It is the strong man who will lend his hand to others, and who lives his life with chivalry and honor."

HPS lights the Protection candle, intoning:
"Come all you Mighty and Unseen,
Who walk all worlds and in-between.
Lend protection on this night,

Grant blessings on this sacred rite.
So mote it be!"

HPS lights the Goddess candle and delivers the invocation she
has written for this occasion.

HP lights the God candle from the Goddess candle and
invokes the presence of the Horned One in a manner he has
created for this celebration.

At this point, an older man enters circle, dressed in green
or brown robes and wearing an antlered crown. He approaches
the boy, as the Horned One invocation ends, saying:

> "Behold the face of the Horned One, lord of for-
> est and of stream. God of the harvest and the
> hunt. Gaze upon me, and behold yourself."

He indicates with a palms-down gesture that the boy is to kneel.
Boy does so.

> **Horned One:** "Young man, I bid you reflect upon the stag,
> for he is the image of our God, known by many names.
> I bid you reach out with your spirit, breathing in his maj-
> esty with each breath. Hear his heartbeat and make it
> your own. Feel his spirit and allow the might and mag-
> nificence of the stag to fill your being. His strength and
> courage lie within you. You need only search within
> yourself to summon his strength. The soul of the stag
> lives in you. Allow the goodness and might of the stag
> to fill your being, dwell within your heart, and guide
> your footsteps on this journey into manhood."

Now comes the time to raise energy. Drummers begin a steady
heartbeat rhythm as the Horned One continues to stand and
the boy continues to kneel. The pattern and pace increase until
a wild, pulsing thrumming is heard, reminiscent of the blood
surging through one's veins.

At the peak of power, the Horned One raises his hands and the drumming ends. He motions the boy to stand, then turns to the Watchtower of the East, saying:

"Gatekeeper of the east, what gift do you bring
to offer? What blessing from the element of air?"

The male representing air steps forth with incense, answering, "I give you the gifts of vision, freedom, and flight." (If desired, a fresh block of charcoal may be lit in the thurible and some of the incense burned, that all may savor its fragrance.) The boy accepts this gift, and places the jar on the altar.

Horned One: "Gatekeeper of the south, what gift do you
bring to offer? What blessing from the element of fire?"

Fire steps forth, blade outstretched upon his hand, and answers, "I grant to you the gifts of passion and of courage. May you be ever the healer, as well as the hunter." The boy accepts the blade, and places it on the altar.

Horned One: "Gatekeeper of the west, what gift do you
bring to offer? What blessing from the element of water?"

Water steps forth, a bowl of spring water held between his hands, and says to the boy, "I bid you drink deep of the Well of Wisdom, which lies within us all. Know your gods, know your Craft, and know yourself." The boy accepts the bowl and drinks deeply, then gives the vessel back to Water, who replaces it on the altar.

Horned One: "Gatekeeper of the north, what gift do you
bring to offer? What blessing from the element of earth?"

Earth steps forth with the bag of seeds, answering, "I bring you the gifts of balance and respect. As the great oak falls, so the seedling grows . . . thus it has always been. Tread the earth with reverence, for it is your sacred home." The boy accepts the bag of seeds and places it on the altar.

The Horned One declares to the people, "_____ is a man today! Welcome him into your circle as such. Embrace him for his wisdom, admire him for his courage, and aid him on his quest."

The new man and the Horned One then tread a deosil revolution of the circle, stopping before each participant to receive hugs, blessings, and well-wishes. HP and HPS thank the elements and the gods. The rite is ended and all may adjourn to a feast, if one has been prepared.

Girl's Rite of Passage into Maidenhood

Gather together the young girl's friends, younger girls, female friends of the family, cousins, and so on, as well as a Crone figure if there is one in your circle. The girl should be attired in special garb—either a robe sewn especially for her for this occasion, or an outfit that makes her feel "all grown up."

A garland of delicate flowers may be woven before the ceremony, to be presented to the girl in circle by a younger child, symbolizing that she has now grown beyond childhood and is being honored by her peers.

For this rite, the girl should bring with her a once-treasured toy she has since outgrown. This will be gifted by her to a younger child to keep and cherish as she once did herself.

For comfort's sake, and because youngsters do tire easily, this ritual may be performed with celebrants seated, if desired. Blankets, throw pillows, and so forth should be in place before circle begins.

On the altar, place three taper candles in hues appropriate for you. (My personal preference is pastels, so I might select pink for the Maiden, blue for the Mother, and lavender for the Crone.) Also on the altar should be a vial of magical oil chosen by the girl's mother or sponsor, for anointing on this occasion. Flowers are always a welcome addition. Any guests who wish to do so may honor the girl with a magical gift, symbolizing her new maturity and growing state of awareness. Some suggestions might include an amulet, diary, bracelet, stones, or an inexpensive drum or rattle. Quarter candles are already in place, with a smoldering stick of incense embedded in the earth beside them.

Led by the Priestess (preferably the girl's mother or female in a parental role), celebrants line up and enter the circle singing a song the guest of honor particularly likes.

Next, Watchtowers are invoked. As each direction is called, its corresponding candle is lit. Greetings to the quarters should be done in such a way that not only grownups can understand and relate, but also that is meaningful to wee folks as well. Examples might be:

> "We ask your blessings here, O Watchers of the East. You whose sunlight shines down from the summer skies and warms our days, be with us now and fill our circle with love.
>
> Come join us now, and blessed be.
>
> We ask your blessings here, O Watchers of the South. Spark our imaginations and grant us the freedom to make our dreams come true. Come join us now, and blessed be.
>
> We ask your blessings here, O Watchers of the West. May we always be true to our innermost feelings and intuitions. Come join us now, and blessed be.

We ask your blessing here, O Watchers of the
North. May we stand as tall and proud as the trees,
growing toward the sky. Come joins us now, and
blessed be."

The Priestess beckons the girl to the altar, and declares to all
those gathered:

"This is a day of joy and transformation. _____
[girl's name, given or magical as she prefers] has left
her childhood behind and enters the circle of
women today. Her body is changing, and her
moon blood has come. She is a Maiden now. One
day she may choose to bear children of her own.
Let us honor her time of passage, from girlhood
into womanhood now."

The Priestess motions to the young child carrying the garland
to come forth and place it upon the girl's head. The small one
returns to her place in the circle. The Priestess now turns to the
new Maiden and says, "We honor you with flowers, as the Goddess has honored you with beauty, health, and strength." She
anoints the girl's brow with the sacred oil, saying, "Remember
that you are a child of the Goddess. She will love and protect
you always. Remember, too, that the Lady has three faces. She
is the untamed Maiden, with windswept hair and laughing eyes.
She is the Mother, who gives life and nurtures and preserves all
things. Finally, she is the Crone, the Old Woman, learned and
wise, who teaches us many things."

Now the tapers on the altar are lit by those women selected
to portray the Maiden, Mother, and Crone. Brief words of
invocation should be spoken aloud by each. The mother or
mother figure of the girl should light the "Mother" candle; this
moment is hers alone. This done, the Mother and the Crone

embrace the girl, and the Maiden bestows a kiss on her cheek in welcome.

The Priestess turns to the girl now, asking, "What symbol do you bring of the child that you once were?" The girl indicates the toy she has brought. The Priestess says, "In becoming a woman, you leave a part of your childhood behind. It is time to entrust those little-girl dreams to another, who may cherish them as you once did." The girl hands over the toy to the child she has chosen to receive it, and they embrace. The child returns to the circle, and the girl rejoins the Priestess.

The Priestess says, "Everywhere we look, life is full of transformations. Buds become flowers, butterflies leave their cocoons. Life ever changes and grows. Let us sing a song of becoming." An appropriate chant is led or a favorite recording played.

When this has ended, the Priestess says, "Now is the time for the giving of gifts! _____ has become a Maiden this day and entered the circle of women. Let those who wish to honor her step forth."

Quarters are thanked; Maiden, Mother, and Crone are thanked and their candles extinguished. Circle is opened and the occasion ends in feasting and congratulations.

Children's Circle Casting

This is a lighthearted ritual, perfect for the children's portion of an open circle sometime in the spring. With the help of adults and a few craft supplies, the kids can create simple costumes to depict the elements invoked—e.g., paper-plate masks with string attached can be colored green, orange, what-have-you, with drawn-on scales to represent the dragons.

Wings can be cut out of posterboard and attached in much the same way, to symbolize the faeries, letting the wee ones glitter and glue to their hearts' content. Mermaids might again

the child in us all

be created through the use of masks and wavy designs, a few seashells attached if the children like. Gnomes, of course, will wear pointy hats. You will want one child decked out in each respective elemental costume, and a fifth child to hold a magic wand—which can be created from a foil-wrapped paper towel holder and leftover Christmas garland or perhaps colored Easter grass.

A simple central altar holds a flower, as many jars of bubble soap as there are children, a basket of water balloons if the parents don't mind their children getting wet, and some cookies and punch for refreshments.

Children gather for the circle, and the following elemental invocations, printed on colorful index cards, are read. Elemental dismissals can be on the reverse side.

The faery child goes "flying" around the circle, weaving in and out of the boys and girls standing there, and then returns to his or her place. The faery child says:

> "We call out to the faeries,
> Your wings are light and airy.
> We call out to the faeries,
> To come and join our fun!"

The dragon child dances around the circle in an undulating motion, making sure to shake his or her tail, and then returns to the original place. The dragon says:

> "We call out to the dragons,
> Come with your tails a-waggin'.
> We call out to the dragons,
> To come and join our fun!"

The mermaid child glides around the circle, making swimming motions with his or her hands, and then returns to the original place. The mermaid says:

> "We call out to the mermaids,
> A-swimmin' in your bright wave.
> We call out to the mermaids,
> To come and join our fun!"

The gnome child walks around the circle, scratching his or her imaginary beard and shaking his or her pointy-capped head to and fro. The gnome child then returns to the circle, and says:

> "We call out to the gnome-folk,
> Bring goodies to your own folk.
> We call out to the gnome-folk
> To come and join our fun!"

The wizard child goes to the center of the circle and raises his or her magic wand, turns slowly all around and points it at each child, and then at the sky and at the ground. He or she says, "We ask the God and Goddess to come to our circle as well. They are always welcome here." He returns to his place in the circle, and all children say:

> "Now we are a circle,
> We really are a circle,
> Now we are a circle,
> The magic has begun!"

The faery child says, "It is time to blow our wishes to the wind!" Children come forth to take their bottles of bubble soap from the altar. As each child blows bubbles, she or he may say what it is they are wishing for. When this is done, the children replace the bubble soap on the altar.

The dragon child says, "We must leap up fast and high! That's how dragons learn to fly!" Children join hands and jump up, to the left and then to the right, three times.

The mermaid child says, "Now we need to cool down and play." Children come forth to get water balloons from the basket on the altar, and have good-natured fun lobbing them at one another. (The pieces will be picked up afterward, so parents, don't you fret.)

The gnome child says, "It is time for a tasty treat; I brought us something good to eat." He passes around the tray of cookies, and the wizard passes out paper cups of punch.

When the children have enjoyed their refreshments, and the cookie tray and paper cups have been gathered and placed back on the altar, the wizard child says, "It's time to thank our friends, who have come to our party today. All children wave goodbye, as each element is dismissed. The faery child goes to the center and says:

> "Thank you to the faeries,
> We know you cannot tarry.
> So farewell to the faeries,
> Our magic rite is done."

The dragon child next goes to the center and says:

> "Thank you to the dragons,
> Go home now, and no lagging
> So farewell to the dragons,
> Our magic rite is done."

The mermaid child next goes to the center and says:

> "Thank you to the mermaids,
> So merrily have we played.
> So farewell to the mermaids,
> Our magic rite is done."

The gnome child goes to the center and says:

> "Thank you to the gnome-folk,
> You fed us well, that's no joke.

So farewell to the gnome-folk,
Our magic rite is done."

Lastly, the wizard child goes to the center and says:

"We now release our circle,
No more are we a circle,
We now release our circle,
Our magic rite is done."

The wizard child says, "God and Goddess, stay if you can but go if you must. Our love and thanks go with you. Blessed be." Children blow kisses as Deity departs.

Bedtime Blessing

Twinkle, twinkle shining star.
Always remember how loved you are.

February

March

April

May

blossom & bower

June

July

August

September

October

November

December

January

Love Song for Pan

In Springtime, I sought him,
Buds burst and sap ran
And my feet found new thawed earth
Went searching for Pan.
I'd heard his sweet piping
One day on the hill;
My heart at once yearned and danced
I hear it still.
By Beltane's bright bonfire
I waited for Pan,
Half-mad with the wanting
Of no mortal man.
But it was Midsummer when
Pan at last came
To me burnished and breathless,
And whispered my name.
Hearts hammered, blood pounded
As flesh joined and burned;
We coupled in soft leaves,
The season soon turned.
And now with Midwinter's
White breath on the pane,
I wait for the greening
To seek him again.

My birthday is May first, Beltane. As a child, I always knew when my birthday was drawing near because the grassy stretch at the side of our gravel country road was filled with violets. Dandelions cropped up everywhere; red buds and dogwood and flowering pears were in bloom. My favorite aunt came bearing armloads of fragrant lilacs from her yard—deep purple, lavender, and white. I was in heaven!

In May's chapter, I present workings to honor a tree and to seek blessings from a fountain. This time of year, the beauty of the natural world abounds and sends our senses reeling.

We urbanites who call the city our home can call on the power of rain to renew and recharge us, in a seemingly unlikely place—the shower! Take down your hiking stick, enjoy the scenic beauty of this trail, and don't forget to smell the dogwoods blooming.

Cup of Joy

Rain is liquid life, a great metaphor for the downpour of abundance into those thirsty areas in our own lives. The showers of spring and the giddiness of the new-greened earth, as she wiggles and stretches and yawns, are a sure-fire equation for luck galore. There is no better time to share a drink and go dancing with the goddess of kismet herself. Here's to Lady Luck!

This spell begins with any truly beautiful container that you can consecrate, drink from, charge, and later use to hold a deluge of happy coins in a sacred space in your home. You may wish to incorporate the crafting of the vessel itself into this working, seeking out a ceramics shop where you can glaze and fire a personal goblet. My love and I found a glass drinking horn on an Internet auction site. Whatever you choose, it should be worthy of sharing a drink with one incredible lady. Her name is Bona Dea, but she has also been called Lady Luck, Dame Fortune, Fausta Felicitas, and Ops, from whose hands opportunities and opulence come.

Do not court her willy-nilly, for she disdains the half-hearted. However, if you woo her sweetly and sincerely, you will be amazed at the blessings that flow through your door.

Next, select a liquid libation that delights both your eye and your palate, remembering that this Lady has class. It need not be alcoholic, although a good wine, sweet mead, or imported ale would do. If an exotic fruit-juice blend from the nearby organic grocery beckons to you, Bona Dea will like it as well. This goddess always has one eye open for adventure.

Now clear off a place in your home that will hold your Cup of Joy. Remove all mundane clutter nearby, so that it becomes a place your honored guest's spirit might abide. Break out your finest candlesticks, newly polished and gleaming, and pop a pair of gold-colored tapers in them. Between them set the best bouquet of flowers your pocket or your garden will afford.

Lastly, select a piece of recorded music that makes you think of sweet serendipity, of lucking into something and being surrounded by richness and satisfaction. Pop that CD into your boom box and cue it up.

Light the candles and cast circle in your own words and way. Pour the beverage and raise the cup in both hands, saying:

> "I drink to thee, Dame Fortune! Lovely Lady Luck,
> I would secure your favor! My heart is grateful, my
> spirit is bold! I seek all the abundance my pockets
> can hold! I toast to my blessings in store!"

Drink deeply, recounting out loud your memories of past strokes of great luck, good timing, and unexpected breaks that have come your way. The Lady likes to know that her efforts were appreciated.

Say aloud, "The world is full of good favor and felicity! My eyes shall be open to perceive the blessings, my heart will remember the kindness. Bona Dea, grant that this Cup shall never run dry. Fortune's Lady, please tarry with me."

This is the time to hit the button on your boom box and let your song begin. Feeling not a bit shy, give Chance an elegant bow and reach out your arms. Pull Possibility close to you, holding Abundance against your heart. Take Ops for a few turns around the floor. You may wish to serenade her, if your tune has words, so croon along. Fortuna will love the flattering attention.

When the music ends, pick up the cup again and announce:

> "This shall be my Cup of Joy, filled with a rain
> of gold and silver coins gathered from the mer-
> riest corners of the earth, until it overflows. May

my prosperity and happiness never run dry. Bona
Dea, bring gold like grain. Bona Dea, shower blessings once again. Luck and love and silver and gold,
all that the heart and the pocket can hold. Bona
Dea!"

Save a bit of libation to pour on the ground later in offering to
her, and for Goddess' sakes, don't be stingy. Once I sparingly
poured a few drops of mead on a rock, only to have the flask
tumble over a few moments later and liquid go gurgling out on
the ground—I had not been generous enough.

Thank Dame Fortune for honoring you with her presence.
Blow her a kiss as she heads toward the horizon, and tell her
you were enchanted to make her acquaintance and you hope
she will not be a stranger.

Rinse out your Cup and place it in the shrine you have prepared. Whenever you find yourself somewhere particularly
high-spirited, where you are treated like royalty, save a few
coins from the chance that you spend in that place. Place them
in your Cup. If friends go on vacation to faraway reaches, ask
them to bring back coins from the cantina where they laughed
the heartiest or the pub where the music was so sweet it made
them cry. Know that as your Cup of Joy fills, its gold and silver
essence is that of abundance and pleasure, the nectar of the
soul. Never spend the coins in that Cup. When your Cup over-
flows, transfer the hoard to a new receptacle—perhaps a small
wooden chest that you decorate yourself. It is working. Keep
your heart and hands open, and good luck!

Shower Power!

Do you love the sound of rain and the way the freshly charged
air smells vibrant and new? If no rain is in the forecast, don't
despair. Step into your shower and call to the "rain" at hand. I

discovered this rite one morning when the day that lay before me was loaded with many tasks. A little rain and a cloudy day has always made things easier for me, and so I step into my shower and call some down.

If you are a shower singer, take a second to think of a song that mentions rain. This can be anything from a classic rock song to the kindergarten song about that old man snoring. It doesn't matter. The important thing is that it puts you in a "rain" space and time.

Say something like, "I call to the spirit of the rain to keep me open-minded and to perceive good possibilities today. Keep my intuition high." Thrust your face under the water for a moment and wash it.

Next, soap up your chest and say, "Spirit of the rain, grant me a heart full of courage this day. Grant that in all ways, I become healthier, happier, and more whole." Rinse off.

Travel down to your belly and lower regions, saying, "Spirit of the rain, grant me this day a bellyful of laughter and a belly- ful of blessings. I know both lie in store for me today."

Stick your feet directly under the stream of water, ask- ing, "Spirit of the rain, grant that my footsteps be eager and unafraid as I walk toward the good things in this day."

Turn now, so that your back is to the water and say, "Spirit of the rain, grant me the strength to shoulder the work of this day alone. Grant that I remember to stand tall and proud."

You're going to love what you do for your back! Take a sec- ond to sway from side to side or dance in place a bit. Then say, "Spirit of the rain, even the willow tree remembers to bend. Make me resourceful and resilient in the day ahead."

Next, let the water cascade down over your hips. The prayer here is, "Spirit of the rain, grant that I remain rooted in sacred space and let none tear my power from me this day. Grant that I stand firm upon the earth."

Turning to face the water again, hold your hands beneath it, saying, "Spirit of the rain, grant that this day my hands are kind and creative, capable, compassionate, and healing. So mote it be!"

Sing a refrain of your rain song (it can vary from shower to shower), end your bath, and towel off lighter of heart and ready to start the day. Another great thing about this working is that if you occasionally use hair conditioners that take three minutes to work, that's just about the amount of time you need to call down the rain.

A Tree-Honoring Celebration

Here is a rite to honor a tree you love. Choose a park or a great green space where the beauty of spring abounds. Set up a picnic for later, then gather your folk in procession, with Priest and Priestess in the lead and those with drums and other instruments bringing up the rear. All who can should wear blossoms, or bear them on the way. The Priest carries a jug of water, the Priestess a small basket of birdseed. It should be noted that on this occasion no ritual blades or sharp objects should be present, as similar things have been used to cut and wound the earth.

Circle your tree three times, then stop. Gently place the flowers on the ground where you stand. Your circle is defined. The Priest steps forward, places his hand on the tree's trunk, and says:

> "Friend tree, we honor thee. Thanks for thy beauty, thanks for thy shade. Thanks for prayers spoken, thanks for vows made under thee, friend tree. Blessed be."

He then takes the jug of water and pours a bit around the tree's base, saying, "As the rains of heaven nourish thee, so we in turn are nurtured by thy beauty. Accept from us this libation." The Priest may then voice aloud any personal pledge to the earth, handing the water to the nearest in circle, and so on around the circle, finishing with the Priestess.

This done, the Priestess steps forth, saying, "Sunlight and starlight and promise of spring, haven to all those who soar and who sing. Friend tree, a gift we bring. Please accept our offering and love. Blessed be." The Priestess pours out a mound of birdseed on the ground, near the tree's roots, and returns to the people.

She says, "Feel now the stirrings of the earth! Witness the rebirth of spring and feel your soul take flight!" Offering the basket of remaining seed to participants around the circle, she asks, "What dreams have you to cast upon the wind? What hopes will you speak in this sacred place? Speak the seeds of your dreams, but hold the seed in your hand until we shall offer it to the sky." Priestess and Priest speak their dreams last, each taking a handful of seed.

Priest gestures for the circle to move closer to the tree and says, "Friend tree, great are the gifts we receive from thee. As the planet turns, and the great earth spins, we feel your energy, drink it in. And now we give back to thee."

A toning begins, energy builds and grows. As the cone of power peaks, the Priestess shouts, "Now!" and all fling their seed upward, into the wind. People place their palms upon the tree to give excess energy back.

Now is the time to hug and feast, to dance and celebrate. May the winds of spring blow gently, and all your dreams come true . . .

The Grandmother Tree

Her heart was hollow, but her branches scraped the sky. Thus it was with the Grandmother tree, a sycamore I believe beckoned the three of us closer that Sunday afternoon. Three friends had chosen Labor Day weekend to leave the city behind. Rippling waters called to us, the promise of nearby wilderness spurred us on, as did a chance to see some stars in an unobstructed sky. And so we began our journey up to Seven Springs Road, past the city of Cave Creek in Arizona.

The Dryad flitted off into the woods, happily "other-where." The Healer unpacked her bags. Every leaf and vine brought back to camp was scrutinized, analyzed, categorized, and verdict rendered to our newly-enlightened *"aaahs."* The Gatekeeper set up camp, scoped out the ground, discovered a stone circle, and met our neighboring campers—all in one afternoon.

The Grandmother called to each of us as tent poles were stretched into place and coolers lugged up from the car, but it was the Dryad who found herself face to face with the tree, hearing her anguished pleas. Her hollow trunk, large enough for three children to sit in comfortably and play "clubhouse," had been packed with garbage. Bottles and broken glass and bulging white kitchen bags crammed the space inside. Some earlier campers had looked around for a dumpster and decided she was it. Her heart was breaking; the Lady felt ashamed and aggrieved and made her sorrow known.

The Dryad placed cleaning out the tree on her list of essential things to do—but somewhere after seeing real crawdads and acquiring interesting rocks. Suddenly she found herself flung into action. A sturdy stick was found among the trash, and debris was dug out, bagged up, and hauled away. The Lady began to smile.

About that time, the most wondrous thing came to be! A red Jeep Cherokee pulled up and a father and two young sons disembarked. The kids drew closer and asked the Dryad, "Why are you picking up trash?" "Because I'm a Witch," the Dryad replied. "And because this tree is embarrassed to have all that junk inside her."

The kids digested that, then hesitantly disclosed that they had seen "a really scary movie" about Witches. The Dryad smiled and asked, "Have you ever seen *The Wizard of Oz?*" Both boys nodded. "Do you remember the good Witch who kissed Dorothy to keep her safe?" Two heads bobbed up and down. "Well," the Dryad finished, "the Witches I know are like that, and this tree is a friend of mine." She went about her way, gazing fondly from the hill's height at the family, now nestled comfortably among the Lady's roots, spending time together.

Evening came, and the call to circle was strong among us all. A cairn was built, and altar set in the holiest place of all—inside Grandmother tree. Out came our candle and jar, set atop a large slate stone, into whose face wandering waters had carved the rune Laguz: feminine energy, the rune of flow. The effect took our breath away; the inner chamber of the tree was lit with faery fire!

The Gatekeeper drummed on the hollow trunk, energy soared. The Healer poured fresh streamwater upon the Lady's roots, and offered up a prayer that all children who might come there would do so with respect and love. Tears coursed down the Dryad's cheeks as she placed three silver coins carefully 'neath the altar stone, a token gesture of friendship and restitution. A small but powerful thing. White zinfandel was shared among we three friends as we found our souls summoned to hear the Lady's tales throughout the night and to honor the seasons of her love.

Our jar candle glowed 'til morning; the memory burns still. A few years ago the Healer was diagnosed with hereditary cardiopulmonary disease. Our last camping trip together was to Seven Springs. The Dryad drove close enough to the Grandmother tree to let the Healer, wearing her oxygen mask, shuffle the few steps to the tree. It was bare of debris, she happily reported. Then the Healer pulled a bag full of round glass pebbles out of her pocket. On them she had laboriously painted runes and stars and words of peace. The Healer bent down with effort and scattered them inside the hollow trunk.

"But kids will just come along and carry them away!" I protested from the car.

"That's the whole point," the Healer wearily smiled. "That's how magic grows."

On the Healer's birthday (she has passed to the Summerland), I, the Dryad, remember her. Since I can bake no cake for her, or help blow out her candles, I drive to the Grandmother tree and honor her memory there. Trees never, ever forget . . .

The Dryad Speaks

I am comprised of autumn leaves,
The drop of an acorn
And the smell of the sweet wet earth.
I have gathered rainbows,
Braided goldenrod
And worn a crown of snowflakes in my hair.

March

April

May

June
tying the knot & untangling

July

August

September

October

November

December

January

February

Handfasting Prayer

Marry me under a garland of stars,
Conifers silent witness
To night wind's echoed vows.
Bearing our promises upward
Through the universal whiteness
To the sepulcher of God.
Touch me once for all time,
All lives that are to be.
Our love enshrined . . .
Marry me under a blanket of stars,
Celestial concourse bless our joy
Now and evermore . . .

J une is the month of marriage. The core of our human experience is the forging of intimate bonds with another human being. The whole world looks on as we move closer, define who we are to one another, and join our lives together. No movie about falling in love is complete until the couple marries and we get to break out the tissues. The bride and groom become King and Queen and take us all, as royal celebrants, along in gay procession.

Not every love fits a fairy tale though, and sometimes those who love must part while there is still admiration and mutual respect between them. Sometimes an ending will lead to an unexpected reunion and remarriage. As a priestess, I have seen the road to love take unexpected twists, turns, and detours, with everyone ultimately arriving where their heart and head seem destined to be.

In this chapter you will find rites honoring that full spectrum, from handfasting to handparting to a rite of reconciliation. God and Goddess bless them all.

The poem at left has been all around the world. I submitted it to an obscure Pagan newsletter two decades ago under my first public Craft name, Larkspur. Imagine my amazement when a young couple in Washington state asked to have it read at their wedding and told me, "We found it on the Internet. It was posted by someone in Sweden!"

Handfasting Ritual

Although most of our families come from traditions in which a single clergyman must be present, such an arrangement need not be the case. I have endeavored to provide a marriage rite in which one or more clergy may preside. I use the term *officiant* to mean singular or plural, and I have omitted words like *bride* and *groom*. Love springs forth in new forms every day, and the gift of the gods is genderless. Honor your day in your way.

On the central altar you will need: gold and silver tapers for God and Goddess (if the celebration will occur outdoors, hurricane globes as wind shields are a good idea); a unity candle, if the couple wishes; and a tray of fruit slices should be covered and available for closing the service, along with a supply of cider, juice, or wine. Choose an appropriate incense for use in the ceremony. You may want a vase of roses, perhaps one fully-bloomed and one yet to open, symbolizing love in bloom and that the best is still to come. Elemental altars should be set with flowers and symbols most suited to that element in place.

Guests are smudged, embraced, and welcomed to the occasion. All are now seated. The circle is cast through the use of spoken elemental invocations that the representative of that quadrant has written. Define sacred space through the deosil scattering of cornmeal or tobacco in the north, birdseed in the east, rose petals in the south, and spring water in the west. God and Goddess are invoked by the officiant, using invocations the couple has helped to write that are unique to their tradition.

Next, drummers who have been chosen beforehand, one stationed in each elemental area, begin a heartbeat rhythm. When it is felt that the energy has reached its zenith, the HP/ HPS raises a hand and signals for the drumming to stop.

The officiant faces those assembled and declares, "Two there are, who would join their lives this day. I bid the lovers come forth."

The couple approaches, each flanked by an attendant who will speak on their behalf. The officiant asks those about to be wed, "Who comes by the grace of the gods, to enter this temple of love?"

The couple answers by announcing themselves thus: "I do, I who am _____." (Magical or mundane names may be used for the purpose of the ceremony; however, the license must be signed with the couple's legal names.)

If the couple is wearing ceremonial swords or daggers, these are now solemnly handed to the couple's attendants as a manifest sign that this is a place of joy and peace. The couple stands open and honest within the sight of the gods.

The officiant anoints the couple one by one, saying, "In the name of _____ [*each one's individual patron deity*], I bless you."

The officiant tells of love, its power and diversity, and then asks, turning attention to one attendant, "Who speaks for _____?"

That attendant answers, "I speak for _____," and gives a brief testimonial that love exists between the two. This exchange is repeated between the officiant and the second attendant.

The officiant hands the gold God candle to one celebrant and the silver Goddess candle to the other. Together, they light the unity candle, saying in unison:

"Be my lover, my companion
Be the guardian of my heart and the keeper of my dreams.
Be ever my true friend.
Share this moment, share my life.
Wherever the gods may lead us, we are One."

The officiant asks, "Are there symbols of this devotion?"

The couple answers, "There are rings we would give to each other today, tokens of our love."

Rings have been held by attendants, who now offer them to the officiant, who blesses them thusly:

"Be thou bound by love alone.
Love is the gentlest of things, yet most enduring.
Love is the sweet spring rains and the crash of ocean waves.
Love is candlelight and forging flame.
Love is the forest cathedral and the tenderest new green bud.
Love is the scent of blossoms on the wind,
And the rejuvenating winds of change."

Rings are exchanged. The officiant now bids the couple to join hands. The officiant holds up the handfasting ribbon, braided of colors the couple has chosen, and shows it to the guests. The officiant explains the significance of each ribbon, stating the attributes the couple has ascribed to each hue. For example:

"Scarlet is the color of courage. You bear it now as you step forth to proclaim your love for one another. May it ever be thus. Guard this treasure well, for you have found the rarest rose.

Turquoise is the treasure of the ocean's depth. May you find much richness in the joining together of lives.

Purple is that special magic between you that grows only sweeter and stronger over time. May there be ever the mystery that binds your hearts together.

Silver, the Goddess gives. The Lady's light has led you to each other. All acts of love and pleasure are her rituals. May joy and laughter, tenderness and mercy dwell ever in your hearts and weave throughout your life with one another.

Gold, the Horned One gives. May strength, courage, and fortitude be at the core of your union together. The world is not always as we would wish it; therefore, find a refuge and renewal in your love for one another. So mote it be."

The officiant binds the hands of the couple together and then turns to the guests gathered there, holding the couple's joined hands high. They are presented as newly wed and are introduced by whatever names they desire. The couple kisses and jumps the broom.

The tray of fruit and supply of wine or cider is brought forth, with the officiant saying, "Let us savor all the sweetness of this day! Blessed be!" Reception and gifting may follow.

Tying the Knot ... I Dos & I Don'ts

I love getting handfasting requests! Of all the rites of passage a priest or priestess can preside over, weddings are my favorite. Excitement fills the air. The couple are so glad they've found you, and they're gushing and glowing in anticipation of their special day. You take down names, dates, and contact information, and so the exchange of energies begins. What do you do now?

Check your parameters. Before you sign on to do handfastings, put your name out there in the public domain, or get your online ordination from the Universal Life Church, you should decide which boundaries work for you. How much lead time do you need, not only to get to know the couple but to hammer out any scheduling conflicts that may arise at your end closer to the wedding time? A torchlight ceremony at seven p.m. on a Friday night may sound divine, but if you get off work at six that's not going to give you any transition or time for dinner, nor an opportunity to shower or slip into garb. If you are able to leave work early, all may be well. Otherwise, you may arrive frantic, disheveled, and frazzled from rush-hour traffic. Would it be better to pass?

Are you willing to travel? What if the couple has elected to have their vows spoken in some national park two or three hours from where you live? If they can provide transportation or lodging, does that still work for you? There might be a rehearsal the night before if the wedding is medium to large in size and complexity. Can you accommodate that as well?

Consider the working time frame you will need to put your part of the celebration together. My rule of thumb is that a couple must contact me two months before the wedding. We then set up a first face-to-face meeting, to get some sense of the sequence and tone that they'd prefer. Subsequent communication can occur through phone calls and e-mails. A month before the wedding date, we all meet and go over the ceremony we have crafted together and make any revisions. Having eight weeks to prepare ensures that everyone is working together, and all parties concerned know what the end result will be.

To every rule there is an exception. A wonderful young couple contacted my husband and me three years ago, in order to have us perform their ceremony over a long weekend. The fellow was due to be discharged from the military and wanted military insurance and other benefits for his love and her children while he could bestow them. They e-mailed us their photos and came looking for us at a Craft camp-out. A hundred event guests, along with the couple's close friends, came to witness their vows and to wish them well. Joyful tears flowed like mead, and it was one of the most unforgettable, sacred experiences of my life.

Handfastings are not about you. Check your ego at the door and set about the task of co-creating a ceremony with the couple that reflects what they'd like their perfect handfasting to be like—usually on a budget. Sit down over coffee and really listen to them. Tell them you are honored to be chosen to share their special day, then let them describe it to you. Too many folks, traumatized by years of "Churchianity," are under the impression that the minister knows best and that the couple has no say in the matter. Encourage the lovers to explore and express their wishes.

You will be called to serve in unexpected ways. I have arrived in garb, in time to coax the anxious, sobbing bride out of the bathroom (yes, it really does happen) and to braid daisies into her mother's hair. Another couple opted to join their lives on a flat rock ledge that towered over a plummeting chasm. Due to my fear of heights, I stood facing the couple with my back against the drop-off. Eeeek!

Let there be something for everyone. Be sensitive to the mix of guests and spiritual backgrounds that will be present. If the couple wishes to be "Craft Lite," tone down the God and Goddess or specific deity references in favor of more universal terms—i.e., Divine Creator, Eternal Spirit, and so on. Crafty folks will sense exactly what you're doing and be fine with it, and such terminology leaves the image of God/Goddess open to interpretation for more conventional souls.

One way to be spiritually inclusive is to weave in a benediction at the beginning of the ceremony, and ask for a moment of blessing on the couple and the loved ones gathered there. The couple may have a favorite reading or prayer that would work perfectly in this portion of the ceremony.

Do not expect to get rich. Before you ever take the first handfasting phone call, determine what fair fee you expect in exchange for your energy, time, and service. If you decide to charge a set amount, let the couple know that up-front. If you opt, as I did at first, to accept donations, you will be pleasantly and uniquely surprised. The first handfasting I priestessed, I was gifted with twenty dollars in cash, a raw garnet, and a handful of porcupine quills. The bride's father was shamanic, and to him this strange hodgepodge represented a tank of gas for me as well as protection and aid in finding a love of my own.

Reserve the right to say no. It is inevitable that you will be contacted by a couple who present logistical nightmares, or whose energies just flat-out make your underwear creep. Don't go there. As respectfully but as honestly as you can, decline the honor and suggest they look elsewhere, perhaps contacting a local New Age shop for referrals.

I have turned down two handfasting requests for darned good reasons. In the first, an agnostic woman was betrothed to a neo-Nazi skinhead man. They looked up a Witch because Christians wanted nothing to do with them. As a woman of Nordic tradition, I cringed at their racist beliefs. Then another theme emerged. The bride-to-be had chosen a park and commissioned her dress to be made. When the groom finally returned one of my many calls, he grunted that he didn't know where the park was, but he "guessed he'd find it the morning of the wedding." I called the bride and offered my condolences, and just said no.

In the second case, I was contacted not by a couple but by their best friend, who had decided it would be just dandy if his friends got legally hitched on the anniversary of their first date, two weeks from the time he called me. He was going to single-handedly make it happen. Uh, weird. And again, no.

tying the knot & untangling

Expect the unexpected. Every wedding has glitches that test everyone's ingenuity. At my most recent handfasting, floral garlands were left at the bridesmaid's apartment, the power went off in the park (no batteries in the boom box, so no lovely Celtic music), and the caterer forgot the silverware. Still, spirits were high and joy filled the day. In lieu of the CD that couldn't be played, a jaunty raven perched in the tree overhead and merrily croaked and cawed throughout the ceremony. The groom's bold mom admonished reluctant diners, "Oh, for gosh sakes, people! Use the fingers God gave you!"

In summary, if you are one of those individuals led to take on the mantle of priest or priestess and participate in such rites of passage, you are honored, blessed, and much in demand. There are great books to guide you, such as the phenomenal *Handfasting and Wedding Rituals: Welcoming Hera's Blessing* by Raven Kaldera and Tannin Schwartzstein, who are also Llewellyn authors. Accept the joy you've been offered, and join hearts together in love. Blessed be.

Handparting Ritual

This rite is intended to be done singly and can be performed by either party. Taking a single taper if you worship only Goddess, or a pair of tapers for Goddess and God, go seek a place alone where you will be undisturbed. Take with you also incense of a calming or purifying kind, the beverage of your choice (you will toast to yourself with this, so make it something good), and two glasses or cups.

One glass will symbolize you; the other, the one who is gone. Your vessel may be anything from your stoneware chalice to the mug you drink hot cocoa from on chilly winter days. The other may be his or her half of a set of wedding goblets, a mug with their name on it, or the like. The object is not nearly as important as the sentiment or memory connection.

Light the incense and ask the elementals to stand witness to your rite. Your words may sound something like this:

> "Watchtowers of the East . . . ease my mind. Strip away illusion and leave me clearer vision. So mote it be.
>
> Watchtowers of the South . . . let anger not consume me. Let me rather use this parting to forge a more powerful sense of self. So mote it be.
>
> Watchtowers of the West . . . let the tears I've shed be healing ones. Wash away my rage and grant me peace that I might grow. So mote it be.
>
> Watchtowers of the North . . . lend me your wisdom. As I reclaim my life and find my balance, I will need your strength. So mote it be."

Light the Deity candles, asking for their presence. In your own free-flowing words, state the reason you are there. Then fill your former loved one's cup with some of the beverage. Toast to him or her: once in praise of any good things you gained through having them in your life, and a second time in praise of any genuinely good traits they possess. Then pour the rest of the liquid in the cup out on the ground and turn their vessel over, saying, "I accept that through your own choices, you have removed yourself from my life."

If you are kindly disposed, and despite the situation all has been fairly humane, add, "I wish you only happiness and peace." If, however, that person has given you nothing but grief, you can add a magical postscript. Have a small dish of sand on your altar, and at this moment say, "Those things you have achieved with honor, may they remain with you. Whatever you have gained at the price of my pain, may it sink through your fingers like sand and mist." Take up handfuls of sand and let them sift back through your hands.

Now fill your cup. Toast first of all to your gods, for granting you the stamina, support system, good friends, and so on to get through this in the first place. Pour out a libation to Deity on the ground. Drink next, generously, to yourself. Give yourself honest praise for those qualities you deem best in yourself . . . your strength, ability to unconditionally love, resilience, and the rest.

End by saying, "I shall continue alone until such time as my heart has had time to heal, and I find love again. Through my aloneness, I shall discover once again the incredible man/woman I am. Through this journey, I shall emerge more beautiful in every single way."

Thank the elementals for their presence, thank Deity for their blessings, and end the rite. Then on all levels, move on.

After the ritual, try to find a way to return the other's vessel to them, through a mutual friend or the mail. Do not destroy what is not rightfully yours. There is one intense exception. I was contacted years ago by a woman who lived in terror of her battering ex-spouse. She received horrific phone calls and was an emotional wreck. She had just performed this handparting rite. Should she look him up to return his coffee mug? she asked. Hell no, I replied! Wrap up that cup in a dishtowel, lay it in the driveway, and take a hammer to it, saying, "I break your power over me!" Bury the pieces somewhere remote. Then I advised her to take legal action. Nothing says love quite like a restraining order.

A Rite of Reconciliation

This ritual is one of reunion, for those partners who love one another but could not live peaceably together, and so they parted. Some essential rightness brings them back together, with clearer vision, more maturity, and the conscious choice to join with one another again.

You will need: two taper candles in colors the couple feel represent them; one white pillar candle to represent Deity; a dish with three slices of bread, two feathers, a chalice, and some wine; a vessel of salt water; and any renewal tokens the couple may wish to exchange.

The officiant welcomes the couple, anoints and embraces each. The circle is smudged and solemnly sealed in whatever manner is appropriate to the couple. The officiant then invokes the elements thusly:

> "Powers of air, you Guardians of the east. Two there are who have come to this place. They are beckoned by the memory of the love they shared together, envisioning that two might rejoin as one. Lend your blessing here, that love might be renewed.
>
> Powers of fire, you Guardians of the south. Two there are who have come to this place. Both were burned by passion's fire yet long for the warmth of one another's embrace. Lend your blessing here, that love might be renewed.
>
> Powers of water, you Guardians of the west. Two there are who have come to this place. Many are the tears that were shed, but still they yearn for one another's kisses. Lend your blessing here, that love might be renewed.
>
> Powers of earth, you Guardians of the north. Two there are who have come to this place. They once were family, lovers, and friends. The road was long and rocky, and they traveled apart, but

now, once more together, they stand. Lend your
blessing here, that love might be renewed."

Invocations to Deity, which have been written by the couple,
are now read by them.

The officiant lights the white pillar candle, saying, "Everything lost is found again in a new form, in a new way. She changes everything she touches, and everything she touches changes. So it is with _____ and _____. They have loved and lost, and sought and found their way back to one another. Blessed be."

The couple places the feathers they have brought upon the altar, saying, "Once love had flown away, fearing itself a captive bird. How empty was my heart, uncaged but still not free. To you I have returned, finding in your arms my liberation and my wings. You are love to me. Let us soar through life together, and be one."

The couple then lights one another's candles, saying, "The dreams we share are beautiful to me. Like rainbows, how they dazzle and illuminate my life! You are the light of my life and all that is brightest and best in my world. I honor you above all others, and acknowledge the Grace that has wrought the rekindling of desire. In the forging fire of love, we are reborn." They embrace.

The officiant hands the couple the vessel of water. They empty it together on the ground, saying, "These are the tears I cried for you, of loneliness and longing, of anger and despair. Although my soul lay parched and bare, in secret love endured."

The officiant hands the couple the chalice, filled with wine. The couple holds it, saying together, "Drink deeply now, beloved, and I will be your strength. Drink deep of love and laughter, of hope and inspiration. Let me give to you the sweetest and best that I can find." They offer the cup to one another, first pouring a few drops in libation on the ground.

The officiant hands the couple the dish of bread. They offer it to one another, saying:

> "Beloved, from the garden of our lives we have plucked the weeds that love might grow again. I promise to enrich you and sustain you. I vow that you shall never lack for comfort, companionship, or love. Accept this simple feast my hands provide." They accept a piece of bread from each other, crumbling the third piece as an offering on the ground.

The officiant asks of them, "Are there tokens you would give, to seal this vow and this reunion?" If the couple has previously exchanged rings, and both still possess them, the rings may be used again. Other choices are limited only by imagination.

HP/HPS then joins the couple's hands together, saying, "You came to this place of your own free will, at the calling of your hearts, to join together once more. Second chances are rarer than rainbows and every bit as beautiful. Treasure this gift the gods have given you, and let no one snatch it away. Protect and preserve this union by your words, your deeds, your honorable intentions, and respect for one another. Love has been renewed and you are blessed. So mote it be!"

Deity is thanked, quarters are dismissed, and the shared journey continues once more.

Wedding Benediction

"Eternal Creator, you who hung the stars in space and set the great earth spinning, you who molded the mountains with your hands, and whose voice whispers to us through the pines, we seek your blessing here. Great Spirit, be with _____ and

_____ on this, their wedding day. May the course of their lives together lie straight and clear, and the rivers of their love run deep. May they always be surrounded by true friends and loving family. May they feel your presence, know your wisdom, and be wrapped in the warmth of your embrace. Amen. So mote it be."

April

May

June

July
one of many

August

September

October

November

December

January

February

March

Healing Invocation

Light and love, to thee I send;
Let the healing now begin.
Heal the body, heal the heart
Let regeneration start.
That every cell grow strong and whole,
Perfect wellness is the goal.
Mend the [area affected], complete repair,
Spirits of earth, fire, water, air.
Gather close and bring [him/her] peace,
That all discomfort soon might cease.
So mote it be!

No matter how much of a magical recluse we may choose to be, there comes a time for each of us to join our energies together with others toward a common cause, or to seek out the company of those of like mind. We add our voice, efforts, and energy, and enter into community. We may opt to become part of a coven or seek entrance into the core group of an open circle. An all-call for a community working, such as a group healing, may stir something in our soul, and so we step forth, lend our energies, and commit. This chapter is about joinings, but it also includes a rite of parting from a group. Sometimes affiliations are unending; other times we know when our journey together is done, and we must honor an exit as counterpoint to an entrance.

I have included a rite of amalgamation, similar to an interstellar rite that Autumn, Joad, and I co-authored in our Moon Grove Coven days. Since we are all science fiction fans and ours was not a degreed or teaching coven, we penned a tongue-in-cheek intergalactic ritual designed for adding contacts.

A caveat here: While the ritual was great fun, its double-edged sword was that by its very nature no one took it seriously—especially the dedicants. This led to much confusion and the conflicts of purpose that Autumn and Joad euphemistically refer to as "trainwrecks." Although it was not our way, perhaps a bit of stripping down, trussing up, and having one's quivering gut challenged at sword point makes more of a lasting impression.

I have been both a covener and a solitaire, and I hold that both spheres have merit. Being embraced as you enter a circle is a hallowed thing. When you gaze into the eyes of a fellow worshipper, stranger to your ken, and see your own reflection, you are home.

Healings

It's a curious point in time. Over the past few weeks I've received so many phone calls from folks going in for surgery or medical treatment. One possible explanation is that our bodies are aligning with new energies Gaia is pouring forth, something always accompanied by stress and growing pains. I only know that in this season, the most vulnerable areas of our lives are brought to the forefront so that things may be confronted and resolved.

Thus it was that a group of solitaires recently gathered, placing flowers beside the healing candles on the small yellow towel laid out carefully on my living room floor. Joining hands, we sang healing runes, then spoke aloud the names of those whose needs were known. We lit a stick of incense for each; soon my white Spirit cauldron was filled, as fragrant smoke wafted out into the evening air.

We invoked the Old Ones, the ancestors, and our gods, asking that their hands be fitted around those of the surgeons to amplify their skill. In the following days, good reports came of minimal discomforts and first-try successful repairs. Healing is a bonding thing. The cessation of sufferings brings us close together. We become a family of need and peace.

Rite of Amalgamation

The doorway to the inner chamber the dedicant shall step through is outlined in Christmas lights, symbolizing a vortex. In the next room awaits a chair, one of those old-fashioned tri-colored Christmas tree color wheels, and a simple altar table that holds two star-shaped candles, a dish of salt and water, and a wand. This wand should be really spacey looking, perhaps wrapped in copper wire with a few nonfunctional electrodes soldered to it. The more resemblance to a bug zapper, the better. The dedicant brings with them an enormous fruit or vegetable, symbolizing the juicy essence of their inspiration, wisdom, and good sense of humor.

Circle is cast in the inner chamber, clockwise with the wand. The Priest says, "I consecrate this sanctum in the lineage of all who have gone before and all who shall come after. We stand between the worlds, at the nexus of Mystery. May the elder races guide us safely through the nebula, and on to perfection as we embark on this magical journey!"

The Priestess consecrates the circle with salt and water, even sprinkling a little on the amalgamation chair. She says, "Great Mother, bless this creature of furniture to your service, in the name of the constellations. May this captain's chair be a vantage point, from which all formations can be seen."

Quarters are called, in whatever manner those chosen for interstellar mission have decided upon.

The Priest lights one star-shaped candle and calls out, "Star Father, guardian of the spheres, we chart our course by your meter's light. Lend your unique abilities to this occasion within this circle, as we welcome a new consciousness to this station. _____ [Name of dedicant] is one. We shall be many."

Priestess lights the other star candle and calls out, "Milky Mother, dust of the comet's tail, blaze forth and bear witness in this sacred space as we encounter yet another species. Consecrate this gathering and bless both our separateness and our symbiosis. _____ [Name of dedicant] is one. We shall be many."

The tricolored rotating lamp is turned on and placed a little ways in front of the chair.

The dedicant is summoned forth, and steps through the portal carrying the fruit or vegetable. The Priest indicates that the seeker should sit, and takes the produce from them, saying, "You bear the seeds of all you have been, all you have seen, all you are becoming. We shall feast on your abundance and be nourished by the knowledge you bear. Be welcomed here."

The Priestess anoints the dedicant with oils and touches the dedicant lightly with the wand and then asks, for all members to hear, "Do you wish to become a member of _____ at this time?"

The neophyte answers, "Yes," "No," or "Can I get back to you on that?"—or jumps up and runs like hell.

If the dedicant's response is positive, the Priest and Priestess walk behind the new member and place their hands upon the dedicant's shoulders. The Priest says, "Receive now your extraterrestrial name." If the new member has thought of a campy intergalactic name, he or she may let the Priest know it now, and be introduced as "_____ of the planet _____ ." If not, one shall be diabolically devised for this occasion by calling out the name of some object found growing or lying in the covenstead's backyard and a character trait of the dedicant's. For example, "Welcome, Crabgrass, from the planet Curmudgeon! You were one, now we are many!"

The Priestess says, "All this has been performed well, with tongue in cheek and a smile on our lips. But now it is time to honor _____ 's commitment, and the members of _____ are happy to receive _____ as a member. Behold our sister/brother, who has come to us in perfect love and perfect trust, to join our group and share in the spiritual intimacy that we all enjoy between ourselves. Let us welcome her/him with loving arms." She faces the new member, and indicates with a palms-up gesture that he or she is to get up out of the chair. "Arise and join us, as we celebrate the circuitry of this great starship's interface. You were one, now we are many!"

The great fruit or vegetable is carried into the kitchen and sliced up. Cakes and ale and hugs proceed at this time, then the dismissal of the Powers of the Universe and the elements are done. Gifts may be presented at this time.

As for Me, I'm in It for the Hugs

Pagans are a huggy bunch, no doubt about it. For me that's one of their dearest traits. Nothing is more evident of perfect love and perfect trust than turning to your neighbor in circle and finding a pair of arms ready to enfold you. You gaze into the eyes of a stranger or a friend and find acceptance there, sincerity in the physical affirmation of their earnest wish for your health, happiness, and peace of mind. It is an opening of spirits that transcends surface intimacy. We invite one another in, foregoing in that moment any need to control, diminish, or oblige. We give of the depths of our souls, offering all we are in the circle of our love.

Hugs don't come easily for some. I grew up as the child of a practical German mother and a second-shift-working Caterpillar Tractor Company dad. Hugs stopped at our house when I turned six, the school bus pulled up out front, and I got on. Without ever intending to, I had suddenly become too old for that physically demonstrative "kind of stuff." All my life, I have envied those souls who have the sensitivity and grace to know when to lay a hand on your arm in conversation, or the proper moment to draw you close in an embrace. For me, it's been a learned art, though thankfully not a lost one.

The Goddess calls a welcome to the child within us all, reconnects the fractured parts, and makes us whole. It is she who extends her arms to shelter us, cloaked in the guise of faces and forms we know. Touch in circle is a holy thing.

Although I am always gratified, moved, and blessed by Pagan hugs from heart to heart, my most memorable experience with sacred touch involved whispers and laying on of hands. At a workshop on sacred trust, women were instructed

one of many

july

to think of one thing we each yearned to do, achieve, or become.

We counted off by ones and twos—the "ones" becoming seated listeners, eyes closed. With soft instrumental music playing in the background, the twos stood behind each seated person in turn. Wishes were whispered in the listeners' ears. Sometimes speakers' hands were laid on listeners' shoulders as a thank-you for hearing, for caring. There were tears in that room; the experience was profound. When we changed places, and the twos became the speakers, eyes were still misty and some voices quivered. As many acknowledged afterward, it was the first time we had ever trusted enough to speak our dreams out loud.

Touch can be in silence, speech, or song. I attended one full moon ritual where the High Priestess taught us all a simple sung chant, then stood before each of us in turn. As her fingertips marked the crescent on our foreheads, and we continued to sing the melody, her rich, clear voice rang out with the descant harmony. Like human tuning forks, we stood vibrating energies against one another. That circle thrummed with indescribable power.

Connecting with one another physically in circle means dropping your own barriers, worries, and cynicisms. You must trust that you are worthy of holding someone else against your heart, that you have the courage to sustain them and the openness of spirit to accept the embrace they offer in return. Two halves of a whole unite, keep multiplying all around the circle, and a bond is formed that never totally disappears. The Goddess sees mirrored in us each aspect of herself, and gathers us together one again. Hugs are the unfolding of our hearts; they are thermal and impenetrable, hallowing and invincible. What more magical gift can one give?

one of many

Arbitration Ritual

Offered here is a ritual I hope will not be needed often. However, even sometimes in the best of circles, conflict between individuals or factions does occur. This may be one realistic, humane, and magical way of dealing with the issue, reopening communication for future growth as well.

Sandalwood incense is lit by a moderator, whom we shall call henceforth *the Veiled One* (VO). This individual's focus is to clarify what has been said by the opposing parties, and to keep the process moving. The VO should never attempt to steer things in a direction of personal interest, as that may not mirror the wishes of those involved. The VO is robed and lightly veiled, as the name suggests, for the sake of ambiguity and unobtrusiveness.

In addition to the thurible, you will need two candles—gold and silver—to honor the God and Goddess on the altar. A shallow bowl, preferably clear, contains consecrated water. Rainwater or ocean water is best, but you may also use spring water from the grocery store and add a sprinkling of sea salt while invoking blessings. This bowl should be of a size easily held between two hands. A pot of earth sits nearby, along with a small green plant. This should be something benevolent in nature, such as aloe, rosemary, or the like.

The VO calls to each party in turn, by whatever names they have chosen, magical or mundane, and bids them: "_____, come to the circle and find justice here."

Each participant voluntarily lays his or her athame on the altar as they enter. On a magical level this signifies each party's willingness to stand unarmed in the presence of the gods, and to open themselves to justice. On a practical level this is not a ritual in which weaponry would be welcome or advisable.

When all have entered the sacred space, the VO invokes the quarters thusly:

> "Guardians of the air, be with us here that memories of peaceful times may temper the times of pain.
>
> Guardians of the flame, be with us here that our passions might do no further damage; let anger and rage not destroy.
>
> Guardians of the ocean waves, be with us here that the waters of understanding might wash our spirits clean.
>
> Guardians of ancestral earth, be with us here that the truth might stand apart, and reason bring balance once more. So mote it be!"

God and Goddess candles are lit, and deities of your choice may be invoked. Any that are associated with emotional healing, clarification, or justice would be appropriate.

The VO takes up the vessel of water, handing it to the first person called into the room, and instructs that one:

> "Speak truly, from your heart, of the time of trouble that has come between you and _____ . Here, in the presence of the gods, let your words bear honor and your feelings freely flow. None shall interrupt you until your words are done."

That individual shares their retelling of the occurrence. Then the VO takes the vessel back, handing it to the next person with the same admonition as before. This is repeated as many times as necessary to accomplish the telling of the issue. The transformative magic taking place here is that the feelings of hurt, anger, mistrust, and so forth are flowing into the water, being relinquished by each person.

Finally, the vessel of water is replaced on the altar by the VO, who turns to the people assembled and asks each of them in turn:

"Is it your wish to continue the knowing of one another?"

If the answer is no, the VO says, "Then in the names of the Lord and the Lady, I bid you leave your grievances here, and depart this place as strangers. Let it be as though you had never met. Take up no word or weapon against one another, but go your separate ways in solitude and peace. Do you swear by the gods to do this thing?"

A pledge is extracted from each one present. The VO takes up the water, pouring it slowly into the pot of earth. Quarters are dismissed. God and Goddess are thanked for their presence here and asked to bless each one involved, keeping the injured parties ever mindful of their vow against further malice or harm.

Participants depart, with the VO saying, "May you know relief and healing. The blessings of our Lady and her Lord now go before you."

If, however, the answer is yes, that despite this time of conflict the parties wish to continue working together, the water is poured out. The green plant is then passed by the VO from one to the other. The VO asks each party in turn:

"What must change, before this peace can be?"

Each one answers honestly what they would ask of the other—e.g., respect for their differences in magical approach, cessation of gossip, and so on. No one is interrupted until the speaking is done.

The VO replaces the plant on the altar, and recaps simply what has been said:

> "_____, it has been asked by _____ that the _____ cease.
> In exchange, _____ pledges to _____ ."

If the initial conflict appears to have been successfully resolved, and compromise achieved, the VO instructs them to join hands and repeat, one to the other:

> "_____, you are my equal and my ally. In the presence of the gods, I offer you respect and trust that you will deal honorably with me. Let there be peace between us now."

Quarters are dismissed and the Lord and Lady are thanked for their presence, as well as for the understanding and communication that has occurred. People now depart; the rite is done.

You Can Go Now

My friend Tyresius has a wonderful custom. When a relationship runs its course and paths must part, he throws a joyful party! Ty will deck out his house in candlelight, and have favorite foods and pastries and some liquid elixir to drink. He breaks out his best incense, puts on some upbeat music, and opens up his door. He beckons his imaginary guests inside, then shuts the door again. To anyone watching, it looks as if he is talking to himself and you might think old Ty has gone and lost his mind. Nope, he's talking to the essence of the invisible guest he's invited to his home that night. There may be only one, or a handful of invitees.

Tyresius pours a goblet of his finest vintage, then talks at length to each unseen guest. He thanks them for their presence in his life. He may laugh out loud remembering fine adventures, pranks, and bad jokes shared. He tells them each what they taught him, and how he is changed forever for having known them. Ty will fling open his arms, as though embracing the one before him. He may bear-hug the air for several seconds, even plant a kiss on a transparent cheek. Then my buddy Ty will open up his door, wave his honored guests out on their way, and say to them gently, "You can go now." He believes that whenever possible, partings should take place in peace.

Group Parting Ritual

Preset the altar with Deity candles, elemental representations, and quarter candles. For this working, use a bell for the calling of air, as vibrations echo through the air and leave as lasting an impression as the words exchanged among members. Incense may also be burned, however, to solemnize the event. Suggestions for combinations include sage, sandalwood, dragon's blood, rosemary, and lavender.

The coven Book of Shadows lies on the altar, as well as any objects the departing member has contributed to the coven and has requested be returned. (Objects have been placed in an inexpensive, tasteful basket or box, which will go with the departing one.) A green potted plant or a seedling tree is also on the altar. This will be used to invoke north, and ultimately be gifted to the departing one.

If the parting is amicable and that member wishes to be present, the ritual proceeds with their participation and ends with thank-yous from continuing coven members and wishes for the departing one's continued success as their spiritual journey unfolds . . .

Each member, for this occasion, has brought a taper candle and holder, which they will carry lit into the circle and place upon the altar at the appropriate time. The candle should be one whose color and design best represents themselves and the particular area of illumination they lend to the coven. The departing one should also bring a candle, as should the Priest and Priestess, whose tapers are already lit and in place on the altar.

The sacred space is smudged by the Priest. The Priestess anoints the members waiting to enter the circle, charging each:

> "May you know only clarity of thought and purity of intention within this place. Enter, Sister/ Brother and blessed be."

All enter the sacred space. The Priest invokes air (by ringing the bell three times), saying:

> "Powers of the eastern sphere, come impart your wisdom here. Let there be clear communication of mind and heart and will. We ask your presence among us. Blessed be."

The Priest next takes up the sword and invokes the quadrant of fire, saying:

> "Transformed by might and forging flames, we feel the power of growth and change. Through union and separation our journeys unfold. We seek your presence among us. Blessed be."

The Priestess takes up a vessel of water and salt and invokes west, saying:

> "Like rivers to an ocean, we are drawn. Some return to source, while others carry on. No loss is without gain in life's dance of joy and pain. Powers of water, be among us now. Blessed be."

The Priestess lastly takes up the green growing plant or seedling tree and invokes north, saying:

"What's formed in love and trust, stands strong. In kinship did we once belong. Powers of earth, remind us of the worth of all that has passed between us. Blessed be."

The Priest lights the God candle, invoking the Merlin:

"Teacher, seeker of truth and knowledge, we seek your enlightenment here. Shapeshifter, transformer, you remind us that we see through many visions, take on many guises, and learn from one another the lessons of the spirit, mind, heart, and will. Help us to grow through this transition. Be among us, Wise One, and blessed be."

The Priestess lights the Goddess candle and invokes Cerridwen, saying:

"Lady, cauldron stirrer, revealer of ourselves, we seek your compassion here. We feel the pangs of change, of dying and rebirth, and strive to see the pattern emerging. Lend us your perception, maturity, and depth as we embrace the new, arising from the ashes of the old. Be among us, Wise One, and blessed be."

The Priest takes his candle and formally announces himself, declaring, "I am the Witch known as _____ , and the light I have carried to this place is the flame of _____ " (indicating the quality he feels he has brought to the coven). He replaces his candle on the altar.

The Priestess takes up her candle and does likewise. She then gestures to each member in turn, who announce themselves and place their lit tapers in a circle on the altar, surrounding the Priest and Priestess's candles. The one who is leaving goes last. All, including the taper of the departing member, are now burning bright.

The Priest beckons the departing member forth, saying, "_____, you have stated that you wish at this time to continue your quest alone." [*Departing member affirms.*] "Your memory will be cherished, although your _____ [*particular gift, attribute, or talent that member has brought to the group*] will be missed. We honor your decision, and may blessings follow you."

The Priestess says, "We thank you for the illumination you have brought to this group, and bid you good journey as you seek your spirit's course. Go now in peace."

The departing member extinguishes their candle flame.

The Priest opens the Book of Shadows and the departing one signs their name in the book, along with any parting blessing, special wishes, or thanks to the coven.

The Priestess offers the departing one the growing plant or seedling tree, pledging:

"As knowing you has nourished us, know that should you call upon us, we will be there in turn to strengthen you. Blessed be."

God and Goddess are thanked, and quarters released. Hugs are exchanged and the gathering concludes on a note of good will.

Version II—If the departing member does not wish to be present, or if conditions of hostility prevail:

The ritual is performed as written, with the exception that the Priestess states that the departing one has voiced an intent to leave the coven. There are brief statements by the group members about the talents/gifts that the individual added to the group. The Priest then extinguishes the flame of the taper candle he has brought to signify the departing one, omitting the pledge of assistance and support.

The Priestess inscribes the name of the one who is departing and the date of the parting ritual. If belongings still need to be returned, this is accomplished with as much neutrality as possible. In this event, the plant or seedling does not go to the departing member, but rather is planted at the covenstead or at a special magical place in the wild, signifying that the group will continue to flourish and grow.

Trees Know

It is only mankind
Who sees in diversity, division.
Trees know no such folly or pretense;
What nourishes one enriches all.
No tree forgets his own kind.
In the sighing of the trees
Breathes the living memory of all
On whose leaves the sun has ever shown.
It is only man who stands alone.

May

June

July

August
claimings & namings

September

October

November

December

January

February

March

April

Litany of Becoming, by Rowan Wakefield

By sacred rite, by candle flame
By moonlight blade and worthy claim
I take to me a name.
Standing proud, I shout aloud
And cast aside all shame.
Nor formed by man, nor father's clan
Nor grandmother nor mother.
Not lover's lie, blood ink to dry,
That bound me to another.
But one that speaks of who I am
And who I've come to be.
I plant the seed of word and deed
And birth my destiny . . .

August is about claiming our power . . . to end a time of terror and to break any self-imposed restrictions that prevent us from being healthy, happy, whole, and moving forward. I once priestessed a Warrior Moon, where a smoky quartz crystal was passed from person to person, instead of a talking stick. We spoke of what was worth speaking up and speaking out for, personal battles we had chosen to fight. When circle was cast, we invoked justice and courage deities, and banged our staffs on the ground for emphasis.

August also seems destined to be the month we lay claim to things and call to them by name. Many ancient peoples were superstitious about others knowing their true name—lest that one assume power over them—and so such peoples always gave a false appellation when pressed. Fake IDs have been around for quite a long time. Among old Germanic folk, the colorful litany of kennings for each of the gods was lengthy indeed. The name we assign to a person, place, or thing matters greatly.

If there is a name we grow to love more than the one bestowed on us through another's blood, a name that declares who we most fully are, then by the gods, let us claim it as our own. My friend Rowan Wakefield has written a beautiful litany of becoming. Make the day you go to court to change your name become your Naming Day. Each anniversary, sign your name to things that are honorable, positive, and that you are proud to stand behind.

'Tis said that before you can leave a thing behind, you must first bless it. Therefore you will find in this chapter a working to break the chains we forge for ourselves, whatever names they bear. Before a bane can be halted, a name must be put to it—hence my working to halt a rapist, which will work equally well for any communal atrocity. Lastly, there is a working to call upon Crow, who is omnipresent this harvest time of year, for truth in all its varying hues. Let us name names!

I Call to the Storm

Years ago I unintentionally called a loved one to me by name, one who made a drastic difference in my life. One dust-storm night in Phoenix, with the sky flashing and distant thunder crashing and unshed rain hanging heavy in the air, I opened up all my windows and doors. I lit incense and candles and implored, "I call to the storm, to enter here and revitalize what I have lost. My heart has become guarded and remote, and I call to the storm to quicken my senses and make me alive again. I call to the passion and the power of the storm, to come and dwell herein!" I enjoyed the windy night and the rains that eventually came, and thought no more of my request.

Two weeks later, as the editor of a local Pagan networking newsletter, *Journeys*, I received a phone call from a lady who wanted to voluntarily submit an article about her experience of being a telephone psychic. Whoa—rare opportunity, that. Usually I had to wheedle, coax, cajole, and downright beg to get folks to write. I arranged to meet her for supper at Denny's, where she would bring a rough draft of her narrative. I was so rattled by her offer that I forgot to ask her name.

When I walked into Denny's that late summer night, the restaurant was filled. I only knew I was watching for some woman with a notebook. Then I spied this lovely, dark-eyed creature, and would've known her out of a crowd of a thousand. Somehow we were already kin. She smiled, stuck out her hand to shake mine, and said with a hint of an Arkansas twang, "How d'ya do, I'm Storm." I kept returning to hug her, again and again. The spark that leapt between us blazed like lightning.

And yes, in due time, she came to dwell with me. Jeweled blips of fairy lights flickered around our bedroom ceiling. My household gnomes amused themselves, and freaked out Storm, by winding up a musical toy unicorn in the middle of the night.

Crank, crank, went the winding key, and the theme from *Babes in Toyland* tinkled for over an hour.

The gnomes had a grand old time stealing the pocket change Storm left lying on the kitchen counter, and ferreting off the tiny crystals and stones she chose at rock and gem shows. As a hoped-for end to her frustrations, and to effect a truce, we set up a special "gnome dish," a new lead crystal ashtray we lined with velvet and in which we deliberately put a selection of shiny things, theirs for the taking. Nope, that went untouched, and Storm's stashes continued to disappear.

Proof of the gnomes' existence came about when we moved a large living room chair to vacuum behind it—and there was this perfect little mound of trinkets, coins, and stones! Storm swears more ingeniously than anyone else I've known, and let me tell you—boy howdy, did she outdo herself that day! Another time she came home sick from work and lay down on the couch. When I arrived, hours later, she told me that she'd opened one eye in time to see a "little guy all in brown and green" just standing there, staring at her.

Storm brought me back to laughter, love, passionate living, and magical existence. Once, to see some snow, we drove to Diamond Point, up near Payson, Arizona. In a bowl-shaped depression, a skiff of crunchy whiteness lay on the ground. We cast a simple circle, seeing the auras of the pine trees extend above their boughs and reach up into the sky. Both of us independently saw the same Crone come walking up from behind the line of trees. She seated herself on a boulder and silently watched our working. She wore buckskin, had eyes as black and bottomless as night, and a myriad of wrinkles were upon her feathered face. When I asked silently who she was, I was told, "I am Nokomis, Algonquian earth mother." What did she want from us? "Feed my children," was her reply. In other words, remember not only the humans but the creatures of the earth. Animal spirits watched us get into Storm's truck and depart.

Storm and I, although separate entities now, have deep affection for one another. I have watched her power unfolding, from the first tongue-in-cheek "chocolate ritual" she attended with me years ago, to coming into her own as a writer, teacher, and priestess of many years. Her Arizona coven, AmberRaven, has a stellar reputation in the community, and a rigorous training designed and mentored by Storm herself. She is a force of nature. I'm glad I called to the Storm, and I'm glad she chose to answer.

Breaking Our Chains

This is a self-releasing, empowerment-claiming group ritual that can best be done at waning moon. You will need: a bundle of raffia and a bell in the east; a bowl in which a mixture of fragrant herbs and dried petals reside and may be given to seekers in the south; a set of runes that may safely be submerged in spring water in the west; cakes and wine in the north; participants to staff the elemental stations and offer elemental invocations; sacred drummers to maintain the heartbeat of the experience; and a rattle to pass from hand to hand, in confirmation of blessings already on the way.

People enter through the southern gate, passing by the fire that is lit by this time, and the abalone shell of smoldering sage. Enter, chanting:

> "Ease our mind,
> Free our soul.
> Unlock our spirits,
> Make us whole."

HPS: "Sometimes, it is we who shackle ourselves. Through our fears real or imagined, our uncertainties and doubts take hold. Sometimes our bonds are forged of complacency, inertia, or doubts that we are worthy of more. We forget that we are children of the Goddess and the God, and that their love surrounds us. We forget that the Universe provides, and that the wise man or woman inside us knows only perfect timing, perfect love, and perfect trust. We forget to relinquish what is old and no longer serves a purpose. We fail to reach for what we need, to heed the inner call, and be reborn . . . "

HP: "Tonight, at waning moon, we shed our old skin and break the bonds that we ourselves have fashioned. We will begin by blessing and purifying this place, inviting our watchers, gods, and guides to stand witness to our rite of transformation."

HPS: "Drummers, now become the heartbeat of this place, and all creation. Echo through our blood and bones. Be the calling, that which spurs us on. Be the balance, that which connects us to all life. Be the voice of all unseen."

Drummers take their places around the four stations . . . as the drummers decide, one by one, that their tie of binding and loosening has come, one of the people who has completed their journey steps up to take the drummers' place so that the beat is uninterrupted.

Quarter calls:

Air: "In this windswept hallowed space
Winged ones, come and lend your grace.
Bless with vision, heal our hearts
As some things end and some things start.
Hail and welcome, and blessed be!"

Fire: "Bright ones, burn away all mundane dross,
Old restrictions, shame or loss.
Leave us gleaming, forged anew,
Strong and bold, strengthened by you.
Hail and welcome, and blessed be!"

Water: "Ocean's womb, from whence we came,
Call to each of us by name.
Reveal to us what needs to be,
Transformation and liberty.
Hail and welcome, and blessed be!"

Earth: "Mountains of the Mother's breast,
Place of comfort, place of rest.
In your refuge, let us stand
Heart to heart and hand to hand.
Hail and welcome, and blessed be!"

Goddess invocation: "O, Great Mother,
You are the answers sought and found in the darkest
hour of night. You are Wise Woman, friend, eternal
companion, and guide.
Come now, to counsel and to bless!
We call to you as witness to the breaking of our chains!
We call to you to midwife this time of rebirth!
We pray you, join us this night.
Descend, we pray you, into this, thy Priestess.
Come now, and blessed be!"

God invocation: "O, Great Father,
You who are the true friend forever at our side.
It is you who teaches us which battles are just,
When we must speak out for another,
When we must reclaim ourselves.
You are our teacher, brother, and guide.

Be the stout staff we lean on,
Be the unfailing heart, wise head, and far-seeing eye.
O, Great One, we pray you, join us on this night.
Descend, we pray you, into this, thy Priest.
Come now, and blessed be!"

HP and HPS bless the cakes and ale, which are later taken to the northern table.

People join hands one by one, saying as they do so, "Separate but united in our hopes and in our fears, we stand as one people. The circle is cast!" The HPS instructs all those present to envision a glowing dome or rainbow light overhead, below, and surrounding the sphere in which all stand. A toning may be used to raise protective energy.

When this is done, the HPS turns to the people and says, "Before you lies the journey. In the east, you may contemplate those bonds you have placed upon yourself. What constricts you? What impedes you? Look into the mirror, light incense to carry your prayers on the wind . . . then take up a length of raffia and wrap it about yourself. It is this and nothing more that holds you back from claiming your true destiny and fulfillment. When you are ready, ring the bell and journey on."

> **HP:** "Next, approach the southern fire. One who guards the holy hearth stands vigil there, ready to cut the needless cord that binds you to your former self. Cast off your old chains into the fire, gaze into its heart, and be reborn. Into the hand that is empty shall be given blessing. Cast your offering to the flames and rejoice that by your choosing, you are free."

> **HPS:** "Then, approach the Well of Wyrd. In its watery depths, distant and unseen, are runes . . . a symbol to

guide you on your way. Engrave them on your mind and your heart, then cast them to the waters once more."

HP: "Finally, come full circle to the healing of the north. Accept the love of the Old Ones, sustenance for the new life ahead, and a message of courage from the God, to speed you on your way."

When all have completed the journey, together again we shall stand. As the rattle is passed from hand to hand, each may speak what he or she has found courage to claim. We shall bless and affirm, by repeating the blessing each one seeks—for example, "We send you abundance! We send you full health! We send you more pleasing work!"

The Priest and Priestess undergo the binding and loosening ritual last.

The God and Goddess are thanked, the elements are dismissed, but watchers are asked to remain until the last guest is safely home.

Crow Season

Crow has left his calling card. Two days in a row, as I strolled past date palm trees, oblivious to all around me, a slim streak of black has blasted me out of my reverie. Sooty Rorschachs, inkblot tests to see if I am listening, courtesy of Crow. His messages are slender, sleek, and the color of jet. I run my thumb along sleek feathers, ruffling the edges. Today, in a supermarket parking lot, there lay a third. Someone else's invitation, whether accepted or unheeded I know not. I gathered it as well.

Crow season means fall is coming, somewhere on the wind. Even though the sizzling Arizona summer may still melt the asphalt underfoot, and to go without cold bottled water is to perish, October is ethereally on the way. It is time to start to hold dear, take stock, and winnow out.

This year, Crow came early. Last year in November, I drove past cotton fields in post-dawn mornings, my eyes delighting in the sight of old black laughing crows, perched gaily atop clouds of white. Salt and pepper.

Some say that to have Crow appear as your totem is to learn the hard lesson of speaking up, and speaking out. Rasping long and loud to draw attention to what is unjust, inferior, and inadequate. Demanding equity, redress, resolution. Crowing about one's own rightful accomplishments and cawing about what we need most, and need no longer bear.

It is not coincidental that Crow made his seasonal debut on the front lawn of my office. Those inky feathers now lying on my office desk are about accepting bare truth, as well as declaring it. I thought of those blackbirds, the now-plowed-under cornfields full of stiff bleached stalks of stubble and hardened clods of earth. Unsolicited intuition came to me, three years ago, regarding a love relationship I cherished and wanted to see grow wings and take to breathless, dizzied flight. Crow whispered instead, "This year is for breaking ground. Next year is the sowing of seeds. Third comes the harvest." Some of the rocks of that first year nearly broke my heart, my spirit, and my back. I admit to second-thinking the endeavor, and very nearly taking to flight myself. The second-year seed time was still tenuous, but I beheld full flower when this third year was new.

Feathers shed remind us what we also must, in rightful time, let drop. A Native American teacher once told me that no bird loses a feather without a drop of blood. So it is with us as well; pruning is not without pain. I weed out my address book, acknowledging ties that have come full circle and have no further place to grow. I ensure that there are plenty of smooth, white pages left for the new bonds that will surely, inevitably come.

A daughter of Crow on the Northwest coast, a provocative poet in rainbow beret, untangled the bonds between us with joy and exhilaration. Standing on a median strip, while cars went whizzing by, Elora kissed me. Then saying, "I release thee," she gave me a wooden cigar box, where inside were layered rose petals, rosemary, and a single raven feather. This was her way of saying, "Remember you are loved, daughter of the north." I never saw her again, but I open that cigar box now and then and smile, remembering.

Under the date palm tree that guards my office door, the trio of grackles I call "the Aunties" gather and kvetch about life. This has been a drought year and their spindly legs and ragged, thinning feathers reflect this. Like some neighborly coffee klatch, they shuffle and peck at the ground, seeking some morsel to share. I set a mental tab to bring in a baggie of birdseed to go with their morning gossip someday soon. After all, it may well have been the Aunties who tipped off the ravens to deliver my love's drinking horn. Quite a story there!

The website eBay is not without its pitfalls, although it never lacks for allure. Amidst oohs and aahs of delight, I recently stumbled across the drinking horn of a lifetime: a butterscotch-colored horn, all capped and tipped with ornately embossed German silver and a delicate chain to hang it with. Oh, wild whoops of joy when that beauty became my prize! Only one drawback emerged . . . the seller, in Russia, sent the package to my former address of years ago, which I had not succeeded in changing, via PayPal. Oh, anguish! Untraceable.

His apologies in broken English were sincere, but my hopes were dashed. I put in a second change of address, left word with that old apartment office, and heard nothing. Then one morning, my job necessitated interviewing a client who lived in those apartments. As I walked to my car from my office, case file in hand, the Aunties stopped chewing the fat and watched me pass. I drove to my destination, no pull at all to stop by the office and inquire of the package once more. But came a message clear: "You need to park in your old parking place and walk down your old sidewalk." Why? The client was quite a hike from there. The message came again, a nag at my back. I did as I was told.

As I strolled down my old sidewalk, and gazed up at an assortment of wind chimes that hung from my old balcony there, a young woman came bounding down the stairs. Two strangers greeted one another, past and present tenants, and out of my mouth came my wish to recover my parcel. She gasped, then ran back inside, got the drinking horn, and placed it in my hands. I wrapped up my business, returned to my car. High up in my favorite pine tree, a dark winged shape croaked something as I strode by. It might have been "You're welcome."

Is there magic one can do with Crow? I think there is. Crow stands for truth—sometimes pretty, sometimes harsh, but that which must be seen and felt and heard. There are three kinds of truth. The first, "The truth that I must utter," is your own personal truth. This implies speaking out your needs and your heart's desire. It includes alerting those in authority to injustice or wrong treatment you are receiving. Victims have no voice. To find your voice is to find your power. It may also mean expressing an opinion or decision that has been called for from you and is needed, but which cannot be sugarcoated. Courage and conviction are required.

The second is "The truth of those who cannot speak." This is about oppression and the larger sphere, and requires raising your voice for the greater good. This may be via the ballot box, letters to legislators, involvement with or donations to crisis shelters, or other causes that stir your passions. You may find yourself carrying a protest sign for the first time in your life, taking a stance, or making an affiliation known. You are asking that silent truth be heard, understood, and affirmed.

The last is "The truth that is not yet known." This is that occasion when your ears have heard all the facts available, but your gut says, "Does not compute." Some element is missing, or being withheld. You need this missing piece before you can make up your mind and know which actions to take. Call for Crow, and call the Unknown forth.

To work Crow magic, keep an eye open for black feathers during your strolls through forest or field. Gather one of them from the corvid clan. If Raven gifts you, great. Broad, blunt-tipped crow feathers are nifty, too, as are those of other black-birds. They are all one family. Set a simple altar, with a bell for air, a dish of seed, a small container of water, two taper candles, and black feathers. I prefer one black taper to symbolize Crow spirit, and I choose the other in a color representative of the type of truth required. For me, red symbolizes bravery of personal truth; blue is the integrity needed to speak for those who cannot; white manifests unseen truth and calls facts into the light.

Cast circle in your way. Then, after elements and deity have been invoked, light the tapers and take up the bell. Turning slowly deosil, ring it at each corner, saying:

> "I would seek and I would know
> The words to speak, the route to go.
> I am listening, I am still.
> Come Crow, from forest, field, and hill.
> Bring courage! Bring wisdom! Bring truth!"

Seat yourself at your altar and take up the feather. Holding it in your hand, speak honestly and in your own words of the situation about which you wish guidance. Ask that clarification come in the time frame specific to your needs—e.g., by the end of next week, the next new moon, by Samhain, and so forth. State that you are open to hearing the truth or facts required, whatever they may be. Then spend some time in meditation and reflection. Close your eyes and see a tree, wherein sit two raucous crows. One swoops down from his leafy bough, dark wings softly cutting the air, and he lands effortlessly on your shoulder. His round golden eyes regard you—sensing, considering. Then he utters a single word. What is it? Have you heard? Does it having meaning for you?

When you have thanked Crow for his presence and his wisdom, close your circle and blow out your candles. Breath is air; so are the winds Crow is borne on and the currents that carry your wish along. Take the dish of seed and water to the nearest outdoor tree. Pour the water, stating that you will always nourish those who are bearers of truth. Scatter the seed, stating that you will feed the workings of justice. Your rite is done.

In my own home, Crow's gifted feathers adorn a blessing broom, along with a handful of corn, some tiny bells, tawny ribbons, and bright berries. I consider the blessings old Crow has brought, and reckon them vast indeed. My fields are full—solid and substantial, bold and true. All too soon the scythe will fall and the last of the sheaves will be husked and ground. As I stand in the midst of barrenness, I will still be counting crows.

Working to Catch a Rapist

Sometimes in the village, a monster lurks. Feel free, if there is need, to adapt this ritual to your own community, its own situation, and the nature of the crimes committed there.

In Phoenix a serial rapist had stalked, maimed, sexually assaulted, and killed a score of women and men, some as young as twelve years old. His crimes had occurred over a whole year's time and as recently as the week before this ritual was performed. This horror could not continue, and while as Witches we prefer to bless and to heal, there comes a time to yoke our energies toward extinguishing atrocity. On a night not long ago, we gathered.

As people arrived, they were met by a sentry holding a flashlight. This is how ritual attendees knew they had found the proper area. When all were gathered, the sentry rejoined the circle. We spoke of why we had gathered, and the working to be done. A white votive candle was lit in honor of the victims. If their spirits chose, we invited them to join us and guide the hand of justice.

We called the quarters with runes, each one sung three times. Ansuz, rune of communication and signals, was chanted in the east, so that new informants might step forth to aid the police in the rapist's capture and trial. In the south, Kenaz, the torch rune, was selected, so that new evidence might come to light. We chanted Perthro in the west, the dipper in the Well of Wyrd, so that police may receive tips and assistance from unexpected sources, perhaps through our anonymous working and the hands of the gods themselves. Thurisaz was chanted in the north, thorn rune and hammer rune, so that the hammer of our good friend Thor might smash down upon this monster and bring his crimes to an end. Finally, we used the rune Teiwaz in the center, for Tyr, the god of justice.

Appropriate God/Goddess invocations were made. Hecate, the Morrigan, Bridget, and Kali were called, as well as Odin, who loves all women.

The one acting as Priest said, "A monster walks among us who tortures and terrorizes, rapes and kills. We must exorcise this demon from our streets, and render them safe once more. Ours are the hearts that grieve for the people raped and killed! Ours are the minds that are horrified at the deeds that this monster has done! Ours are the hands of justice! The monster's deeds must end! Rapist, your atrocities shall not continue! Your reign of terror shall cease!"

The woman acting as Priestess said, "Let the record of his crimes be read, so that all remember and bear witness!"

A newspaper article about the rapist's crimes was produced and read aloud. Aluminum foil was laid out on the ground, to form a reflective surface. Our sentry with the flashlight moved in, so that the "spotlight" shone on the rapist.

The Priest instructed, "Bring the rapist forth." A poppet, which had been prepared ahead of time with the police sketch artist's rendering pinned to its chest, was brought forth and laid on the foil.

The Priestess said, "Creature of art, be the tool of our will. We name you the rapist, and make you the object of our working tonight. So mote it be!"

The Priest drizzled honey on the poppet, saying, "May you be caught fast, by your own misdeeds. Stuck fast in your own monstrous web of hate and cruelty and death, unable to rape and kill again. We bind you fast until the police can apprehend you, try you, and lock you away. Rapist, your reign of terror shall cease!"

Many in circle sprinkled banishing herbs on the poppet and spoke their own words of exorcism/binding/justice, all ending with "Your reign of terror shall cease!"

When all who wished to had scattered their herbs and had spoken, our Priest said:

"The hand of Justice will hold him accountable
for his deeds. Any others involved in these crimes
will reap swift and terrible justice as well. Let the
monster bear the weight of his misdeeds."

The Priestess said, "Rapist, we see the depths of your perversion and the darkness of your soul. As your deeds have sent our senses screaming and pierced our hearts with the anguished cries of those you have tortured and have slain, so we pierce the void that was your heart. Who will slay this vampire of death and destruction?"

One stalwart soul claimed the honor, and a wooden stake and a hammer was brought forth. The stake was driven through the poppet's chest, pinning down the newspaper article.

The Priest folded the aluminum foil around the poppet and took up a ball of string. The bundle was bound and knotted, while we all chanted:

"Your reign of terror shall not last!
The hand of Justice binds you fast!"

When the string binding was done, a small hole was dug and the poppet was buried and covered over.

Our justice rite concluded with attendees joining hands in a circle and our Priestess saying:

"None of us walks alone. We stand together, in
strength, solidarity, and love. Go in safety, children
of the earth. This rite is ended. Blessed be."

A short time later, an arrest was made and the string of assaults in Phoenix abruptly came to an end. Our streets were safe for a while.

And a Wise Man Spoke

Saying, "Honor the splendid moments of your life.
Name them as the jewels they are,
Cherishing their brilliance and their fire.
Hoard them all the days of your life,
For they are precious beyond all measure.
Those times of cold and dark,
Loneliness and wounding of the spirit,
Name as banes.
Hurl them from you as swiftly as you can,
Let their hardness and their sharpness
Bruise your heart no more.
They have taught their lessons
And are now rubble.
Fling them far from you
And set your spirit free.

June

July

August

September

words of power

October

November

December

January

February

March

April

May

GodSpace

Honored Father, we feel you near us.
Be our counsel, be our guide.
Sacred Father, bless and cheer us.
God of courage, now abide.

Songs murmur what we cannot find the words to speak aloud. A certain tune comes on the radio and we, customarily soft-spoken, suddenly pound out a rhythm on our steering wheel, screeching at the top of our lungs and finding joyous affirmation in "our" song. My mom's single biggest fear, when selecting her funeral hymns, was that she'd likely offend more faint-hearted folks if, in addition to traditional hymns, she included a recording of her favorite "running naked" song. Mom never got to go streaking, but that's okay, Mom—I play the song in your honor every now and then. I sing along on the chorus, and I grin from ear to ear!

In this chapter we honor the power of words, both sung and spoken. Our voices can evoke imagery, create an energy field, or bring a thing into being. In this chapter you will find an honoring ritual for a bard as well as a deflection working for uttering the words that will keep negativity and hidden agendas away from your threshold. Lastly, I've included a suggested working for the moments when no fancy tools or circle props are present, and our words and our will and whatever's at hand have got to be enough. The magic is in you. The Latin root word of *invocation* is *invocare*, which means "to summon forth." Let us breathe our spell into existence.

In Equal Measure

The Craft is, by its nature, matrifocal. The presence of a Heavenly Mother as giver of life, consoler, and renewer is what leads many women, as well as gentle men, to that path. Lyrical Goddess invocations exist in great array, both spoken and sung. In addition to stanzas and prose to honor Maiden, Mother, and Crone, should there not also be praise for the young Stag, the Father, the Mage? At the beginning and ending of this chapter are two that I have penned. Feel free to share them. They may be included in rituals as spoken invocations or tailored musically to whatever tune you fancy.

Blessings for the Bards

I never felt the lack of a bard until the day a circle died. Across a room, seventy-five people clasped hands and stared at one another, uncertain how to end this wobbling, awkward affair. A roomful of Pagan strangers had assembled to celebrate community diversity and had drawn lots to see which factions would write the circle casting, energy raising, and declaration of intent.

No one knew what happened to the group who fumbled the ball at the end, but after a century's pause, one lone voice began bleating out a tired, clichéd refrain. I heard the Goddess groan, "Oh, for Persephone's sake—reruns again!" She snatched up the cosmic remote and promptly changed the channel. A bard could have saved the day and fixed up that fiasco with one chord.

When Leslie Fish, of filking fame, came to call the desert home, I had no idea what a jewel had landed in Arizona's lap. The lady bard and her guitar graced many a circle, asking for little more in return than applause and a drop to wet the whistle. Unthinkingly, few offered more. Only in my travels, when I spoke her name and was treated to dropped jaws and awestruck gasps, did I begin to have a clue. Leslie's CDs can be purchased by contacting her agent Random Factors, and her controversial book, *Offensive as Hell: The Joys of Jesus Freak Bagging*, is available on Amazon.com. Well worth acquiring!

As I researched the role of bards throughout the ages, it became clear that a bard was a hallowed guest. The Celtic bardic tradition dates to ancient times, but was most prominent in medieval and post-medieval Wales and Ireland. Many bards resided in wealthy homes, others were itinerant. They were particularly important in Wales, where bards were often noble, and where bardic guilds were formed to set standards for writing and reciting. Repeatedly outlawed by the English as politically inciting, the institution gradually died out.

In Ireland, the training of a bard lasted twelve years, with students undergoing a rigorous curriculum. In the initial years, the student progressed from "principal beginner" to "poet's attendant." By his eleventh year, he was termed "a noble stream" because "a stream of pleasing praise issues from him, and a stream of wealth to him." Once a bard had mastered three hundred and fifty stories, he was considered a master and was entitled to receive a gold branch with bells attached. When the bard strode into the hall, all were alerted to become silent and summon the help of the inner realms to inspire his poem, song, or story.

Bards were deemed to be prophets and emissaries of the Divine, able to bless and curse with a stanza of three lines. Because of the level of autonomy and impunity granted to bards, they often became the voice of the people, whose tongues had to remain still to keep lives, lands, and families together.

Do bards fulfill those same roles today? Yes, indeed! Leslie Fish's most famous magical trilogy of songs, formulated specifically to end a prolonged drought, brought down a deluge from the skies. Beginning with a tune called "Thunderbird Road," which acknowledged the dry, parched ground, she then shifted into a more up-tempo number that musically pleaded, "More, more, more . . . we need more!" Leslie's rousing finale was a hymn to Thor, entitled "White Man's Rain Chant," which exhorts Thor to "draw the drops of the sky together . . . break the back of burning weather." Works like the weather charm it is.

Yet the lady bard can curse as well as cure. Anyone who hears Leslie, an impressive flint-eyed figure with ink-black hair and a knife tucked in her boot, belt out "The Oathbreaker Song" shudders with relief that the words weren't intended for them!

At circles blessed by bards, rituals flow, segues are apparent, and some high-octane energy gets raised. Bards have an innate knack for weaving people together. At a Yule celebration in Bellingham, Washington, I fretted as the talking stick was passed and the full spectrum from serious believers to scoffers became apparent. Then Dougal, our resident bard, picked up his guitar and sang about finding commonality in the heart of our differences. Suddenly, his strings were not the only thing in tune. As one body, many hands reached for red taper candles and lit the wishing wreath. Camaraderie prevailed.

Is there a blessing for a guesting bard? Not that I have ever come across; therefore, one needs to be created. One might propose the following festive inclusion. Prior to the bard's entry into the hall, two garlanded, gaily-adorned sweepers come with sprigs of laurel, rosemary, and pine (honor, remembrance, and renewal), signaling the people with: "Music comes! The heart string hums! The good bard comes!"

Enter a third attendant with sistrum or cluster of bells, who announces as the bard walks forth, "Hark, they ring! Rejoice and sing! Each shining thing the good bard brings! He/She comes!"

A low-draped table should be set aside, near the comfortable seat of honor to which the bard is led. As the feast begins, food is brought to the bard first, by one who says, "Play for us and touch our souls. Be sustenance, uplift, console. As your music feeds our spirits, may this meal lend strength to your body, good bard."

Drink is next poured for the bard, with this blessing: "We bless each note that from you pours. Your tales are ours, our love is yours."

As the last song is sung and the music fades, a purse is given to the bard that each in attendance has graced with monetary gifts. The gifting words spoken, by the one chosen to bestow the blessing, are: "With gold and silver and precious things, an offering for your blessed strings. As every chord rang bold and true, good bard, we praise and honor you!"

Let us, as Pagans, restore our bards to the esteemed position that from antiquity has been theirs. No longer an underpaid afterthought, but our voice, our magic, and our hearts.

When God Walks in the Room

"Play my song!" the young man begged, stopping just inches away from the lady balladeer. Without missing a beat, she raised her head, looked into his eyes, and smiled.

"I don't know which song is your song," she said, "but I'll play one just for you. Okay?"

The fellow clapped his hands and laughed with glee. "She's going to play my song!" he shouted to the audience, twirling all around. "For me!" The young man's sister, hovering near the door, looked mortified. Bad enough to be left in charge of your mentally challenged sibling for the day, worse still to have him disturb a public concert.

The musician's fingers nimbly picked out the last refrain of the piece she was playing. One last chord hung quivering in the air, then died away. She asked the man his name. "Davy!" he excitedly pointed at himself and grinned broadly. "I'm Davy!" The lady raised her gaze to the crowd; her eyes swept the room.

"This is Davy's song!" she announced, and broke into a lively reel. Davy danced in place and cackled aloud, shaking red curls all around. Moments later his sister crept forward, took him by the arm, and led him away.

The concert continued that September afternoon, with songs being sung on every stage. The Prescott Folk Festival, in Prescott, Arizona, is an auditory feast. One may listen to a cowboy range song twanged out in one place, then stroll a few feet farther, and there's harmonica with fiddle back-up. The friend I'd ridden up with from Phoenix had rendered love songs, protest songs, and finally wound up on the children's stage where Davy walked in.

Next morning over breakfast I congratulated her on having not been rattled by the sudden interruption. She had handled it with delicacy and grace, I assured her, not allowing the disturbance to impair her performance and interfere with the pleasure of her listeners. The balladeer stared at me with a strange expression on her face. A spoonful of grapefruit paused halfway to her lips. She lowered the food, leaned forward, and spoke:

"When God walks in the room, he is your audience. He stands before you, and you play for him. Over the years I've been honored to catch a glimpse of Deity in many a stranger's face."

We ate in silence. I felt humbled somehow, and tucked the seeds away, not knowing when they would sprout. Last weekend, in conversation with a friend, the story came tumbling out. I held it in both hands, examining its worth.

Who can say when Deity enters our presence? Christians are reminded by Jesus, in the book of Matthew, that sometimes the divine arrives in a stranger's guise: "I was naked and ye clothed me, hungry and ye took me in."

Pagan cultures have ancient references to the gods assuming a mortal disguise, to test the wisdom, hospitality, and assistance of a host. Old Scandinavian people put "mead in the drinking place, food in the eating place, and music in the listening place," so that the stranger, whether human or divine, might think on them kindly and bless them and all they possessed.

The Goddess came to me unexpectedly one day at a welfare office in the guise of Myrna, a young woman whose life had been plucked up like a handful of marbles and scattered to the wind. A promised job, family support, relationship, and solvency had evaporated overnight. Yet her faith remained intact. As I snapped her photo ID and lined up what emergency aid our agency could give, I voiced my wish for better things.

Myrna answered softly, "All that will come. My sister-in-law is Puerto Rican. Tonight I will do something she told me long ago. I will go stand outside my apartment and open my arms to the moon. And I will tell her, 'I am empty, Lady—fill me.' And since I have done all I can to make things happen for myself, she will answer and provide the rest. One can only do this when there is truly need." Her belief rekindled my own.

I found the God in my neighbor Bob, with all the failings of the flesh. An older gent with a fused right leg, he sits drinking coffee out at his patio table, inviting the world to stop by. Bob keeps watch, warns of danger, and will share with you one of his stories if you trade him back one of your own. He is the traveler's friend, the innocent's ally, and the foe of perniciousness everywhere.

Bob doesn't miss a thing. He has seen the robed ones emerge from my apartment, sniffed purple clouds of incense wafting by. But he only chuckles and says to me, "We know all about you; you're a good Witch." I have the Hermit's blessing, a powerful thing indeed.

Bards see through different eyes from us ordinary folks. They feel the rhythm of life's refrain. They perceive the pattern hidden in the midst of serendipity. A good bard always knows when God walks in the room . . .

Stop Right There! The Creation of a Hidden-Agenda Detector

Our words can invite, coax, cajole, comprise, soothe, and heal. Our spoken vows are pledges, and verbal contracts are binding in many courts of law. Words can also halt the advancement of a thing or an individual. No pronouncement freezes up our hearts more fiercely than having the boss stride in on Monday morning and declare, "You! I want to see you in my office right away!" Our shins begin to shake and all momentum turns to Jell-O.

Consider this: we have anti-theft devices in our cars and smoke detectors in our homes. Why then should we not have an anti-nonsense deflector right inside our door? Unseen and even decorative, it can quietly send out "walk on by" vibrations to pesky peddlers of door-to-door varieties as well as presumptuous megalomaniacs who think they know how you ought to be living your life according to their plan, and folks with hidden agendas. Now, I am not advising you to ward off loved ones in genuine need. Everyone's life hits a crisis at sometime or another. The difference is that most of us learn from the crash landing, brush off the dust, get up, and go on. Some folks, however, like the sorry scenery so much that they elect to build a condo there. You know the types.

Here is what you will need: one of those fillable plastic ornaments that come in two screw-together halves, available at any craft store; and some very pretty, fuzzy, or shiny yarn for aesthetic appeal and concealment of the real goodies within. Scour your magical books for properties of banishing herbs and stones. Is there a metaphysical shop in your town where you can get your hands on some wolfsbane, a High John the Conqueror root, perhaps a wee bit of black salt and some sulfur? Those will all stop badness right in its tracks. So will cayenne pepper. I always pocket an extra packet of crushed red peppers at the local pizza place and have it handy in my broom closet at home.

Cloves exorcise right well. If there are roses growing nearby, pinch off a few thorns and tuck 'em in for good measure, so that those with dark agendas get pricked by their own guilty conscience and misdeeds. You can't beat a tiny piece of smoky quartz for diffusing negativity and leaving your house's aura fresh and clear.

Now then, head for your kitchen, which is usually not far from your front door, lay out everything on a long piece of foil (a reflective surface), and go to work. First snip off some of that glorious yarn and make a "nest" inside one half of the plastic ornament, forming a hollow where your foil-wrapped ammunition will reside.

Ready? Now, placing one thing at a time on the sheet of foil (you need only a pinch of each for powerful juju), you may wish to intone something like this:

> "At this time and in this place
> A charm I make to protect this space
> From unseen enemies.

A bubble sphere,
A sentry here
Against those who would seek to harm.
With High John's power I raise my shield
And ancient power do I wield
That shall repel each curse or hex.
By nettles might I now diffuse
All whose negativity might choose
To interfere with mine and me!
With salt, I drive all ill away
Back whence it came, and may it stay
Apart from we who dwell herein.
With thorny spike and pepper's fire
I fend off all who might desire
To bring malice to this home.
May not a thing be well with them
Who darkly plot and evil scheme.
Away! Away! Stay far away
From here, where love resides.
So mote it be!"

Whew! That was invigorating, right? Now, wrap up the foil around your pinches of power and tuck the darling bundle into its resting place, nestled in the yarn. Snip off another clump of cozy yarn and fill the empty half of the plastic ball. Now you may either simply screw the two halves together, with a mind toward recharging your ingredients periodically or adding new ones, or hot-glue them together for permanent effect, as I did.

Where do you put this glorious gizmo of yours? Why, almost in plain sight, of course. Mine is rolled discreetly behind my small cookbook collection. That way, if Aunt Jolene comes over to borrow a recipe for the Mennonite potluck and comes across my nonsense deflector, at worst she'll think it's some kind of peculiar pet toy and she'll wonder when we ever acquired a cat.

Magic in the Making

Rituals are like soup starter, even the ones in this book. They merely provide an example of what artifacts one Witch might lay on his or her altar and the magical method that Witch might use to cause a thing to be. Take what's useful—tuck it away just as you would in some mental recipe file. Then know that there will come a moment when the need is immediate, and all the props and pretty words are gone. Those are the moments that your phone rings with news in the wee hours and someone asks for energy. Those are the occasions when a friend requests help with a private working, after other circle guests have gone. You speak from the heart and you take what's at hand, and somehow the magic works.

Need to clear a space unobtrusively, in a hurry? A holiday jingle bell, sentimentally hung on one's keychain, is quite delightful. I moved into a different cubicle at work recently, in which the energy from the previous occupant was frantic, disorganized, and unfocused. I sighed deeply and made peace with my supervisor's choice for my relocation, and then I yanked out my car keys and headed for the now-vacant cubicle. I jingled my keys all around the space, turning to every direction. I voiced that for me, that tiny boxed-in space would be a place of peace, productivity, and joy. No one was the wiser—they just thought Bronwynn was pacing around her new digs with her keys in her hand because she was anxious and upset. Voilà, a cleansing had occurred.

Years ago I received an out-of-state phone call from Aunt Ginny, telling me that Uncle Irwin, who had been laid off from work for several months, finally had an interview. That morning I drove to the top of my parking deck at work. Just me and the pigeons at seven a.m. up on the rooftop floor. I used my car's cigarette lighter to fire up a stick of incense. Then, standing outside my car, I saluted the four directions and poured my heart out to the gods. I spoke of what a hard worker Irwin was and how he had busted his hump to keep belly and back together for his family. I asked that he really shine in this interview today, and that if it was the happiest outcome for all concerned, that the job be his. My small ceremony ended with no flourish or fanfare—just me, Deity, and the birds. Several days later a note from New England arrived in the mail. Irwin had landed the job! The pay and benefits were good. Aunt Ginny thanked me for my prayers.

Know how sometimes you'll get an indication that your petition has been heard by Deity, before the final outcome of a thing is known? Here's a cool tale to share with you.

After an open Samhain circle, my dear friend Elaine and I gathered trash and talked. An avid horsewoman most of her life, Elaine has loved many steeds but none so deeply as Slayer, a seventeen-hand, nine-year-old thoroughbred. A few years ago Slayer took a fall and became injured. His physical deterioration since then has reached a stage at which he can no longer be ridden. Elaine faced two possibilities: the first was Slayer becoming strictly a companion animal to another healthy horse. The second was the sickening reality that she might have to euthanize him.

What sort of work could we do, two Witches alone in a mountain park with the altar and tools already packed up by others and taken home? We brainstormed. Were there oatmeal cookies among the remnants of the feast? Elaine checked and found none. What did we have to work with? She suddenly remembered that she had a small plastic container of apple slices in her truck and went running for those. On the ancestral altar scarf of black and silver, many in circle had earlier placed mementos, before ritual began. Elaine had brought strands of Slayer's hair, from a time of grooming him, as he lay heavy on her heart. The scarf, which I had brought, still lay waiting. We had enough.

Taking the bits of apple, we walked to the ancestral altar and spoke to Epona, goddess of horses. Elaine spoke of her love for Slayer, what a marvel he had been, and of his present plight. We asked the goddess to place her hand on his bridle and to lead him to the fairest meadows and sweetest grass imaginable, and we stated we would trust her knowing ways. Elaine took some of the apples, I took the rest, and we scattered them as an offering to the creatures of the wild. Then we drove home.

A few days later I received an e-mailed update on Slayer from Elaine. Moments later something miraculous occurred. Atop Elaine's e-mail in my Yahoo account popped up a "please pass this on"-type message from a Catholic friend, Ken. His e-mail told of two horses in a field, one with a bell tied to his harness to guide the other horse, which was blind, and of the need to turn to one another for sustenance in times of impairment or despair. The bottom line was, "You listen for my bell and I will listen for yours." I forwarded the e-mail to Elaine and advised her, "Light a candle and say thank you. Epona is striding through."

Within a few hours other options had begun to open up for Slayer. Could he perhaps pull a small cart? Horse lovers from several states had started contacting others to see if he might find a stately friend in their stables and fields.

Slayer's story is still unfolding, and Elaine is considering many loving options. Epona has the reins. Any inquiries can be sent to me and will be forwarded to Elaine, who thanks all for their interest and good will.

Magic is within us, not without. We just need to speak the words . . .

Father in the Coming Night

Father in the coming night,
Keep us safe within your might.
Sage and warrior, horned hunter
Guide us to you.

July

August

September

October
telling the bones

November

December

January

February

March

April

May

June

Bonechant

Old bones, cold bones
Lying in the ground,
Shallow bones, fallow bones
Good to have around.
One to stir the cauldron,
Two to beat the tune
Conjuring the ghastly ghosts
Who march beneath the moon.
Three or four or more suffice
For resurrection's sake
But any more than seven
Is a grievous mistake.
Eight will chase you halfway round
The world and back again.
Nine are best forgotten,
Be you man or fey or fen.
Ten bones go a-roving,
Fingers up and down your spine
Giving little shivers,
Make it difficult to dine.
Mean bones, lean bones
'Neath a broody sky,
Dig them deep and bid them keep;
Let sleeping spirits lie!

There is nothing so fey as October. Leaves decaying under-foot take on the loam of the grave. The woods are a haunted place. We honor our lineage, and try to stop catching our breath and glancing back over our shoulder every time a floorboard creaks or branches scratch like cat claws against our window pane. Samhain is old magic, and anyone can walk into your days and dreams.

One young adolescent October I walked home from school alone, having been sick with menstrual cramps earlier that day. On the asphalt hill no cars went racing by. From nowhere the old woman approached me. A thick, dark coat hung down to her shins, a gray wool scarf was tied under her chin. She came to me, peering intently into my face. "Do you know me?" she asked. Frightened, I shook my head and prepared to run away. She untied her scarf, shook out her curls—once auburn, now streaked with gray. A million wrinkles creased her cheeks and lined her raven-black eyes. "Do you know me?" she challenged me again. I was mute, close to terrified tears. The old one regarded me sadly, and said mournfully, "How could you ever forget my face . . . ?" I walked rapidly on toward home, turned back once to look and she was gone. The Crone came up to greet me that chilly autumn day, but I was young and small and scared. I'll bet you that now we'd have a longer chat . . .

At Samhain, we remember that life and death are twinned. As we walk through the waning sunshine of the year, shadows stretch out before us. We remember those who came before, those whose love remains although their physical form be gone. We think on those never born. In this chapter you will find an ancestor ritual as well as a rite for those who could never be born. In preparation for our own eventual transition out of life to beyond, we reflect on who we are and how we will wish to be remembered.

Ancestor Ritual

This ritual is a "cozy" one, right for the time when the winds grow chilly and the scent of fresh-baked cookies calls each one of us home. Along with your Deity candle, choose an ancestral candle, one whose color evokes warmth, compassion, and pleasant feelings in you. And although it may mean a trek to the corner florist, have flowers for those you are remembering. Have soft incense burning, something subtle and sweet that makes you think of bygone days. Include any other tokens your ancestor held dear. If he smoked a pipe, why not a pinch of cherry-blend tobacco in a little bowl? If an apple tree grew in her yard, warm up a glass of autumn cider so that its fragrance adds charm to your ritual. Photos of your deceased loved ones should also be present, perhaps on a nice crocheted doily.

Invoke the Guardians thusly, tinkling a delicate bell at each quarter:

"Old Ones of the morning birds,
Be with us now, for you are welcome here.
Come now, and blessed be.
Old Ones of the hearth fire,
Be with us now, for you are welcome here.
Come now, and blessed be.
Old Ones of the sweet spring rains,
Be with us now, for you are welcome here.
Come now, and blessed be.
Old Ones of the blossoms,
Be with us now, for you are welcome here.
Come now, and blessed be."

Light the Deity candle, saying:

"Lord and Lady, I invoke you
And invite your presence here.

> May I find within this circle
> The blessings that I seek.
> Blessed be."

Now light your ancestral candle, saying:

> "You who came before
> Are not forgotten.
> Although I can no longer
> Enfold you in my arms,
> You still sweeten my days with memory.
> You walk through my dreams
> And lend me strength when I am weary
> Your love is warmth when the world is cold.
> _____ [*Name of loved one(s)*], come!
> Let us visit here.
> Loved one(s), come!"

Somehow, I've always envisioned this invocation being spoken with one of those wonderful old-fashioned music boxes tinkling sweetly in the background.

Now is the time to remember. Do that in your own way, silently or out loud. Gaze at the picture and imagine yourself sitting across from the one who is gone, hearing their stories once again and telling of your life to a dear friend. Bring up any issues in your life or decisions to be made, and invite their guidance.

Cakes and wine should be a pleasing part of this ritual, and any drink and pastry whose taste and aroma appeal will do. Perhaps a pot of tea and an ethnic pastry, such as strudel, from your own grandmother's lineage?

Thank the ancestors and ask them to leave a bit of their love and wisdom behind. Thank the Lord and Lady and dismiss the quarters. This rite is gently done.

Ghost of a Chance

Samhain gathers her cloak around her, rustling as she goes. Her hands are cold, her visage dark. But those of us who are sighted in the old way do not shrink back in terror. We open our door and ask her in, pouring a bowl of brandy and setting out a plate of supper for the souls who pass in her wake. It is that time between the worlds, when we may catch a glimpse of our own beloved dead. We may be only bystanders as the parade of souls passes by.

My grandmother Anna Edith, she of the gray eyes and coronet braids, left the world laughing when I was only six. She threw back her head at a visitor's joke, her mirth like silver rain. Then she crumpled to the floor and was gone. I went to the funeral, watched my grief-stricken mother trying to force the fairest gladiola from her garden into her mother's stiffened, waxy hands. No resemblance there, between the taxidermied corpse and my grandma in her shoe-top apron, slicing home-made noodles or nursing a runt baby pig with a bottle in her arms. The day after her funeral I rode my bike past her house and glanced up just in time to see her shielding her eyes from the sun, waving to me from the veranda. I waved back, then remembered she was dead and went crashing head over handlebars.

Not all ghostly echoes are benign. As a young adult I attended a Midwestern junior college at which a murder had occurred. Information was tightly capped. Sources would only admit that a woman had quarreled with a man obsessed with her, and had been found dead. Around the campus were extensive wooded trails where the pair had been known to walk. Students trembled and walked to their cars in packs, taking no chances. One wintry night I stopped by the restroom off the large cafeteria, set back into the alcove of the performing-arts room. No one else was around; chairs were racked up on tables, put up for the night.

For just an instant, I saw the white letters of the "Women" plaque on the bathroom door colored in, in red. Vandalism, I shrugged, and went on inside. Although I was quite alone, I could not shake the feeling of someone menacing lying in wait for me. My heart hammered as I stood at the sink, washing my hands. Then I smelled fresh blood, pungent as a nose bleed. Terrified, I hurled my whole body at the door, reckoning that if someone were indeed standing just outside it, I would at least knock them off balance. I hit the parking lot running and didn't stop until I was locked inside my car.

One year later I dated a fellow who had worked at that same school as an audio-visual technician. It being late October, our topic turned to haunts. I shared that tale, and grew pale. "Get off the freeway immediately!" he told me, as we drove. "You need to be off the road when I tell you this!" Puzzled and perturbed, I took the next exit, pulled into a gas station parking lot, and waited for his explanation. You guessed it; the dead woman's assailant had argued with her on the trails, then followed her toward that bathroom after her last class that night. He lurked until no one else was around, then savagely strangled and stabbed her to death.

Sometimes a ghost will linger out of nostalgia, much as we living do, and serve as an unlikely guide. In the ghost town of Nelson, Nevada, stands the remnants of an old bordello, cathouse of mining days long gone by. The front porch is rickety and missing several boards, so be careful where you step. Outer walls have splintered away, letting slivers of daylight seep in. Inner dividing walls are only a bit more sound.

As soon as I had climbed the porch, ducked my head inside, and laid the palm of my hand against a wall, there he was. My mind's eye was filled with an image of a jaunty little fellow, brown hair balding on top. He wore a short-sleeved shirt and a whittled pencil nub was tucked behind one ear. He gave me the impression he'd been a bookkeeper for the mines.

As if through his eyes, I saw visions of how the whorehouse had been. I heard laughter and conversation, the tinkling of an upright piano two rooms away, and I knew where beds busy with more intimate activities once were. And, he assured me emphatically, if anyone gave any trouble to "the girls," miners dealt with the roughhouser pretty darned fast. He shared his memory of a belligerent drunk being dragged off to the entrance of a mine before being given the thrashing of his life.

The chatty little man was still making his presence known as our group prepared to leave. I asked for a moment alone and silently thanked him for the tour. Then I told him he must wait there, to tell the others how it had been. He chuckled, dipped his head in parting, and I went on my way. He's likely waiting still. Perhaps you'll be the next to hear his tales.

This morning I lit jack-o'-lanterns along my balcony wall. I waved to Samhain in the distance. I heard the wheels of her wagon creaking nigh, with whispers and glances and unions renewed. I smiled at the nip in the pre-dawn air and thought to myself, "There's nothing like October to give one's spirits a lift . . ."

Rite for Those Unborn

Every year as we enter the season of Samhain, we celebrate and lovingly remember those cherished souls who have known us and departed. But what of those souls we could not bring through . . . the unborn, released back into the Mother's care?

Sometimes, for one reason or another, things happen to prevent a soul from making its entrance into the world. There may have been a miscarriage, a stillbirth, or a pregnancy that had to be terminated because the circumstances weren't right, or the health of the fetus or its mother was at risk. For some, whose arms are empty and aching, there seems to be no rite of release, no true goodbye. For them, I offer up this rite. There are two variations to this ritual. One is for those who wish to bear a child again, at a healthier point in time. The second version is for those who do not wish to become pregnant again, and who choose to relinquish that spirit in love, and point the way toward other doors through which it may enter the world.

Rite of Release for an Unborn Soul

The bearer and her partner should both be present for this ritual, if it is their mutual decision that they both participate. They should seek out a place by a living body of water—an ocean, stream, lake, or the like. Build a small mound of stones, on top of which an undyed beeswax candle can be placed. Choose purity of color, because the soul did not experience living connections with family and friends nor those circumstances that shape and mold us all. Light myrrh resin atop a charcoal block. Myrrh opens gateways, but it also releases sorrow. It will act as a channel for the soul to pass through. Beforehand, craft a small boat—perhaps out of a walnut shell, seed pod, or other lightweight thing—and line it with herbs, flower petals, or whatever is pleasing to you. Take a moment to ground and center; then light the candle and incense, saying:

> "Small one, the reality of your presence changed
> my visions, altered my destiny, and entered my
> dreams. Yet your time was not to be. I/We could
> not bring you through; my womb could not grant
> you safe passage. The season of your birth must
> wait. I now return you, sweet spirit, to the lap of
> the Lady. With the light of this flickering flame,

I illuminate your way. Do not forget me/us, but pray return in your own best and most perfect time. Wrapped in a blanket of perfect love and trust, I release you into the gentle arms of the Great Mother. Rock gently, tiny spirit, until we meet again."

Set the little boat adrift into the steam where the currents will carry it on. Only when you are ready, extinguish the candle flame and go home.

Rite of the Open Womb

If you yourself have chosen not to bear a child, or have elected to end your childbearing days, you may know of another woman or women who wish to become pregnant. This rite is from you to them.

Go to the green woods, where fertile plant and animal life can be seen in great profusion. The woman or women who wish to conceive should accompany you for this rite. For this purpose you will need a fragrant blessing incense, a seed of any kind, a candle for the unborn child, your athame, and a candle for each of the ladies present.

With your athame, dig a shallow hole in the earth and plant the seed. The act of fertility has occurred. Light the incense and say:

"Blessings on you, sweet spirit! We celebrate your yearning to re-enter this world. Although my womb may not bear you, there are others present in the circle who long for a child. They would greet you with gifts of unconditional love and great rejoicing and provide for the needs of your days. Sweet spirit, I give to you _____ [insert the name of the woman desirous of conception]. She is a worthy mother, whose womb is ripe to receive and nourish you, whose arms in joy would eagerly enfold you, whose heart yearns to nurture and embrace you. Consider her, gentle spirit, should you decide to stay."

The woman named then lights her candle, saying:

"May the light of this flickering flame shine as a beacon to guide your way to us."

Repeat this with each introduction, and conclude after all women have been introduced with: "Rock gently, tiny spirit, as you drift on the Cosmic Sea. May the Mother of all, in her wisdom, let us come to know you soon."

Pushing the Envelope: A Pagan Preparation for Death

We've all heard the horror stories of how someone like Lady Lemuria, a.k.a. Susan Smith, died of a sudden heart attack and was given a private Christian burial by her loving family while her covenmates were still reeling from the news. Although that name and scenario are fictitious, if there are no written last requests from members of our Craft communities, you'd best be resigned to the fact that conventional kin will soon be singing "Amazing Grace." The deceased, who might have preferred cremation, will be pushing up daisies and taking an eternity to make things right with the Lord. Not the Horned One. You know, the other Lord, that guy with the white robe and stone tablets.

What should we as responsible, loving Pagans do for ourselves and for those we will ultimately each leave behind? Moon Grove Coven had a solution that I think would work for us all, covener and solitaire alike. What we each did, at the time that felt appropriate, was to write out any bequests "in the event of," as well as any passages of poetry, memorial tributes we would wish spoken, and so forth. The writing was signed and dated, then placed in a sealed envelope that went into the coven Book of Shadows. It would never be opened or read—"unless."

Although Moon Grove disbanded in 2003, Autumn and Joad still have my envelope.

My Craft-friendly family knows where my books and tools should go when I've left this mortal plane. My husband Dan knows that no stone will bear my name, but a hundred trees from coast to coast will be planted in my honor. He knows where to scatter my ashes, and which oaks will speak to my soul as it pauses and reflects.

Being one gifted with bursts of far memory, I do not fear the Veil or passing through it. As Z Budapest once said truthfully, "It is not death we fear; it is suffering." Here, then, for both contemplation and chuckles, is the scattering ceremony I have written for myself.

When the time of my reaping has come, and direct cremation without embalming has been accorded to me, let those who have loved me take a handful of my ashes and scatter them on the winds, in the place I walked and spoke to the trees and collected small woodland treasures.

Facing east, one says:

> "Odin, Alfather, whom Bronwynn loved, thank you for all the wisdom she and we shared together. Thanks for all the great journeys you led her on, gallivanting all around the Midwest, Southwest, Northwest, and gods know where-all else! Good winds and godspeed to our priestess friend, until we meet again."

Turning to the south, another says:

> "Lady Freya, goddess of love and of magic . . .
> we thank you for all the bawdiness, passion, and
> inspiration Bronwynn brought into our lives. Yes,
> she could be a real little strumpet and quite a pot-
> stirrer at times, but you know—nobody's perfect
> and we loved her anyway. Let her hang out with
> you awhile and hone her skills (now that's a scary
> thought!), then send her back again. We will wait
> with open arms and loving hearts."

Turning to the west, a third says:

> "We honor old Aegir, lord of the sea. Thank you
> for the treasures you laid in Bronwynn's hands, and
> the stories in turn that her nets brought back to us.
> From your mead vat, which never runs dry, we lift a
> horn to Bronwynn, who will ever return to you."

Finally at the north, the final speaker says:

> "To her ancestors she has gone. Bronwynn refused
> to carry a pager and only recently consented to
> owning a cell phone. Knowing her, she'll have it
> turned off for a while, then get back to us when
> she feels like it. She'll be busy collecting rocks for
> a while and adding new nut hulls and seed pods
> to her collection and looking up her old dryad
> chums. They'll have a lot to talk about! We look
> forward to her return."

All present toast with mead, and say aloud as they raise the horn:

> "To Bronwynn, the teller of tales, the Wanderer's
> child, and so on!"

Finally, someone says:

> "Good friend Thor, ready guest at hof and har-
> rowing, today we clap you on your broad back
> and thank you for Bronwynn's vibrant presence
> among us. We thank you for every time she went
> flying into battle to do what she thought was
> right, for those concerned. Yes, we know she was
> a little 'reactionary' at times. No one trusted her
> with the kitchen knives when she got pissed off,
> let alone broad axes or spears, but a shield maiden
> she was, friend Thor, and she did us all proud."

Toasting and reminiscing may continue until all the mead is
gone, the park rangers have come and carted folks away, or
those in sumbel have passed out cold. Remember to plant those
trees. My spirit needs a "guest house" until I choose flesh again.

So . . . a little rest upon the wind, then new tales to gather
in. I shall find you again, dear friends. Here is my envelope, if
you please . . .

Hall of the Grandmothers

I felt so alone. It seemed that life held only disappointments,
rejections, and dreams I had bartered away. Where was the
mother, to listen and to love? Where was the grandmother,
with her wisdom and advice? Both of mine had vanished from
the earth, leaving me orphaned and abandoned.

I poured out these feelings to the Goddess one night, as we
met in meditation. She asked why I was sad, and I replied with
a powerful lump in my throat that maybe I just needed a hug.
She shook her head gently and replied, "No, you need a grandmother. Where is yours, child?"

"She died when I was six," I swallowed, regaining control.
I told the Goddess all that I remembered of Anna Edith, my

German grandmother. I shared the image of her deft hands twisting sheets of colored crepe paper into roses, pansies, and poppies. Those she sold in bunches on a corner in town, along with bittersweet wreaths when the ground had frozen and there was no work until spring for my well-digger grandpa.

Then, needing to retell the tales, I told the Goddess of my mother, dead at sixty-three. Mary Lucy was a practical joker and a collector of bawdy ballads, who regarded K-Mart as her personal sacred shrine. I saw old men with walkers hurl themselves out of the way of Mom's cart when a blue-light special was announced. Mom was loud and lusty and alive. She had been proud of me. Found among the contents of her purse when she died was a finger-worn copy of a poem I'd written for her many years ago. During my starving single-parent years, she slipped me extra gas money. Before her death she had her diamond and sapphire ring sized down for me, so she could see it on my hand. Not a day went by that I didn't whisper "I miss you, Mom," with an awful ache in my heart.

The Goddess asked then about me. My account was a dollop of self-pity, spooned out over a generous helping of "life sucks," but the Goddess didn't flinch. Her voice was soft, her gaze was tender. "The Hall of Grandmothers," she stated solemnly. "Do you know the way?" I shook my head. She beckoned, "Come, I'll take you there myself." I looked away, suddenly ashamed of revealing so much of my heart. The Goddess held out her hand to me, and I took it.

We parted just outside the door. She left me with a kiss upon the brow. "I love you, and I am always with you." She gazed into my eyes for a moment, brushed a hand across my hair, and she was gone. I glanced around. Along a concrete walkway, tulips and crocuses lined up in gay parade. There was a scent of hyacinths on the breeze; lilacs and peonies bloomed.

Two lawn chairs sat on the front lawn, a place where sunsets could be watched and long talks treasured. An old metal swing set, repainted numerous times and worn smooth from a succession of young bodies, sat under a shady tree. For a long time I just stood there, taking it all in. Then finally, without a clue to what I might say to whoever lived on the other side of that door, I tapped lightly and waited for a response.

"Come in, child!" a voice called out. Tempted to retreat, I timidly turned the knob and pushed open the door. A plump gray-haired woman was sitting in one of those high-backed cushy chairs, knitting an afghan in colors I like best, all rusts and greens and golds.

She looked up at me and her smile lit up the room. She laid her knitting aside and held out her arms to me. I knew her instantly, though we'd never met before.

"Come here, Chickadee!" It felt like forever since anyone had called me by that name; I was ten years old again. Unembarrassed, I rushed forth into her arms. For the longest time, the grandmother just held me against her bosom, stroking my hair. Over and over, she told me how glad she was to see me. She smelled of sunshine, strawberries, and satin sachets.

She patted her lap, saying with infinite tenderness, "You're never too big to love." I climbed aboard. Somehow, it seemed I was child-sized again, and that lap was the most comforting place in the world. Without a word, she rocked me, and I buried my heart against her heart, felt all the anguish melt, grateful beyond words to be safe, secure, and cherished. My tears trickled into her hair, but she didn't seem to mind. She just whispered, "Life is hard, child, and sometimes you do get weary. And it's okay to cry, but the trick is not to ever let life beat you down for long. Look . . ."

She pointed to a nearby coffee table, where an assortment of photographs stood. Amazed, I realized that the pictures were of me and those I held most dear. "But how did you . . . ?" I asked her.

The grandmother smiled. "I know you well, child. All your hurts and disappointments, but I know your triumphs, too. The times you risked yourself to see justice done for another, the times you succeeded or spoke your mind, or had the heart to dare what others thought was foolish. I'm mighty proud of you. Go look in that trunk over there." She pointed to a cedar chest across the room, and I slid down from her lap and went over and lifted the padded lid. Inside lay a large three-ring binder, filled with every scrap of poetry I'd ever written—good, bad, or mediocre. I took it out and brought it to her. Together, we leafed through it, and as she asked the questions, I told her the tales. She shared a few of her own.

She kissed my cheek, then went to brew us a pot of sassafras tea. We drank it together. I savored every drop and began to sense that my time here was drawing to an end. "Before you go, Chickadee, why don't you have a look around? It's really a wonderful place."

"Can I ever come back again?" I asked.

She smiled, "I'd be very upset if you didn't! You are always welcome here, and always loved."

With a parting embrace, I left her. Out the back door, I saw an incredible sight.

The yard I had walked through was gone. In its place, a freshly plowed garden patch had appeared. Another grandmother and a grown-up child talked as they planted flower bulbs together. This grandmother was the color of rich, dark earth. A ribboned straw hat was tied under her chin, and her hands wore gardening gloves. The middle-aged man who bent down beside her, and set each bulb with such exacting care, looked as if he might have been an executive. The telltale signs of crises, deadlines, and many nights of burning the midnight oil were etched into his face. But for this moment he was perfectly at peace, and having the most soul-nourishing time of his life.

I walked around the side of the house. Two women, one old and one older than time, sat side by side on the canopied porch swing. The silver-haired grandmother held an antique photo album in her lap; the lacquered finish had cracked in places and some of the pictures had yellowed and curled, but there was a memory behind each one. From somewhere inside the house a piano tinkled, playing long-ago songs, growing-up songs. The elder's eyes outshone any star; the moment was pure gold.

Suddenly I was standing beside the Goddess again. "You're smiling," she observed. "Your visit did you good."

"How can I ever thank you?" I asked.

"Be good to yourself," she replied. "Don't take life so seriously, and dammit—lighten up!"

I gulped! I had never heard the Goddess swear before!

"One more thing," she continued. "The next time you visit your grandmother, you might want to take her some flowers. I understand gladiolas are her favorite."

"Thank you, Lady." I kissed her, hugged her with my eyes.

"You're welcome, child. Blessed be."

Love is Never Lost

Kindness carves an image
That time cannot erase.
Though gone, they walk among us.
Glimpsed in a passing stranger's face.
Or hear a strain of music,
And suddenly they're near.
Feel love and warmth around you
From those no longer here.

August

September

October

November

venerations

December

January

February

March

April

May

June

July

In Odin's Name By Roderick Runesayer, 1992

In Valhalla's shield decked halls,
Heroes raise their horns
To the God Who is Glad in Battle.
I am not there.
At the roots of the World Tree,
I drink a cup from Mimir's Well,
Grateful that Odin paid the price
For my taste of sight.
In the high holds of Kings,
Bright Lords reckon Allfather's lineage
As their own,
Paying homage to His ancient name.
I am not there.
My blood is Othresir, Mead of poetry,
Stolen by the High One's hands.
Find me on the far flung hills,
Talking to ravens.
My life I give on Yggdrasili limbs,
Flesh and bone hung like His,
As an offering for the wisdom of the runes.
My home lies where His path leads,
Be it Asgard's shining hall
Or Hel's frozen depths.
Whatever others have done
In His name or against it,
Faithful He has been and faithful I will be
From Ginnangagap to Ragnarek's flames.
I follow Odin.

There comes a time to acknowledge and revere those of wisdom and integrity in our Craft community, who have grown to the mantle of elder. Through their quest for knowledge and earnest desire to serve, they have become mentors, resources, Wise Ones. We know them by their quiet authority, their unmistakable presence. They bring the circle with them, unseen but tangible. All heads turn when they enter the room; all hearts mourn when they leave this plane. We must cherish them while they are living and tell their tales, so that their legends live on.

There are Merlins among us, and the saging rite in this chapter is to acknowledge them. My croning ritual is a bit atypical, but one I might wish for myself someday . . . hint, hint. Lastly, I've included some suggestions for how to keep the torch of memory lit for worthy crones and sages long after their flame has gone out. The honor of knowing them is ours. Let us celebrate those who shine!

At left is an excerpt from a poem by a mage, whose like we'll not see again. It was offered to me years ago, for a local Pagan networking newsletter, and I have always loved it.

Remembering Roderick Runesayer

Oftentimes in our Craft community, it is hard to tell where the person leaves off and the persona begins. I knew Roderick the teacher and the mage—his antics, visions, and stories. But I wasn't well acquainted with the father, lover, or son. When he died of a stroke in 2003, I and the rest of the Craft community were left with pieces . . . here an image, there a photo or a wisp of conversation. Here is the legacy Roderick left to me.

I met the Runesayer shortly after coming to Arizona from my native Illinois. Experiences with a certain one-eyed god soon netted me invitations to sumbels, blots, and runic drummings. Being in Nordic ritual would often lead to far memory visions for me, and I discovered that Roderick was an excellent sounding board, being second-sighted himself. At an ancestor blot, as the drinking horn was passed, I suddenly wasn't there. Instead, I mentally saw myself in a distant place and time—clusters of women and children, men in the middle. As I watched, two men approached, carrying what appeared to be a long paddle between them. That must be a mighty big vat, my present self remarked. Then a gray-haired priest beckoned them forth, and mead was sprinkled over both ends of the wooden tool—I was recalling an oar blessing.

For a later Desir blot, in honor of the Grandmothers, Roderick brought oatmeal cookies, telling of how he was nudged in a vision to bake them up. In meditation, he saw himself enter Frigga's hall, a wonderful aroma wafting through the air. He sniffed. Aaah, what was that? She answered, "Oatmeal raisin cookies." Where did she get the recipe? Roderick wanted to know. Frigga laughed. "From your mother, of course!" she replied.

Roderick was a rake, a prankster, a scoundrel, and a heartthrob. Cloaked and wrapped in furs, long locks flying and hazel eyes gleaming, he made old women sigh and young ones faint dead away. One year, Roderick entered the sexy-doughnut-eating contest at our Phoenix Witches' Ball. Cream-filled doughnuts were cut in half, lads cued up to display their techniques, and a handful of lusty wenches judged. All I will tell you of Roderick's effect—my face flushed even now in recollection—is that all of us female judges fanned our flaming faces with our skirts and went out for a cigarette afterward—even the ones who didn't smoke!

One late evening I ran into Roderick Runesayer at a downtown bookstore, and we talked the few minutes 'til closing. He suggested we adjourn to his house nearby and continue swapping tales. Fine by me. We kicked off our shoes and sat Indianstyle on his bed, trading gossip. Three hours later I strolled through the door at home. "Where have you been?" my roommate glared, who'd waited supper. "Sorry," I grinned. "I was on Roderick's bed." She didn't speak to me for a week.

Roderick the teacher was a respectful fan of elemental magic, and had done a turn of the Wheel with each energy in turn. He spent the shortest time with fire, as he quickly became impatient and short-fused. He offered a token sacrifice to each element as he undertook the study of it. Spirit was the hardest; he was asked to "take off his hat." What that meant was that Roderick, ardent Society for Creative Anachronism (SCA) member, actor, and icon of a local Pirates guild, had to forego part of his costumery for that sojourn. In other words, he had to be his unadorned genuine self.

Roderick didn't hold with commanding anything to "be here now," reasoning that if he invited a VIP guest to his home, who could break him like a twig, he sure as hell wasn't going to whip open the door and holler, "Hey, Bub! Get your ass in here!" Likewise, he preferred to think of himself as Nordic tradition instead of Asatru, because of the difference in levels of inclusion.

Roderick held that reincarnation explained a multitude of interests and inclinations, and that no earnest seeker should be denied knowledge. His attitude was, "How do I know that the African-American guy sitting next to me in the restaurant didn't used to be Erik the Red?" Likewise, upon hearing that some folkish factions had heartburn with homosexuals, Roderick's stance was, "Hey, if Thor attended a wedding in drag, Odin wore a skirt to go hang out with the Witches, and Loki birthed an eight-legged horse out of his wazoo, there's plenty of room for some gay guys!"

Roderick was an unforgettable wedding priest. One night, while officiating an SCA wedding, he stepped closer to the bonfire, enclosed in a sawn-off barrel, to better read the text. It had rained the night before, and as he slid, he lost his footing. Roderick had only two choices: somersault over the jagged barrel rim and hope to land on the other side, or miss and be gutted like a fish. By the grace of Loki, the Runesayer made it, bouncing upright on the other side, his book still in his hand. Awed wedding guests whispered, "Do they always do that?!" Roderick answered solemnly, "Only in my tradition."

He shared his vision journeys and his dreams. One illustrated the occasional folly of waiting for words of wisdom from beyond. Night after night, Roderick drifted off to sleep, hoping for prophetic utterings. Finally, one night, came an image of a stuffed fish on a stick, rather like a scaly hobbyhorse. As Roderick watched in dream, the fish opened its mouth and spoke. In its best Shakespearean tones, it dramatically cleared its throat and declared, "And the fish said . . . doo wah diddy, diddy dum diddy doo." Hmmm. Heavy, man.

Roderick was the first person to hug me, no strings attached, after a brutal divorce. He held me one night at an SCA gathering in a park—friends for life, feeling my pain. Both of us wept.

As the human vultures and would-be paramours circled to pick my ragged bones, Roderick suggested we join the SCA supper crowd. He hung by my side, noisily gnawing and growling and slurping on rib bones, his cloak protectively draped around the back of my chair. The jackals backed off.

For circle some nights I don a special piece of jewelry, a runic necklace crafted for me by Roderick. The terra cotta rounds are inscribed with the runic symbols Uruz, Elhaz, and Sowelu: strength, protection, and wholeness. There was mistletoe juice in the pigment with which he painted them, magic and regard in the making.

Over a hundred mourners showed up at Roderick's SCA/Pagan memorial service. Bagpipes were played and a drinking horn passed from hand to hand as each spoke their tribute aloud. One male guest whimpered, "Roderick was my friend; he always held my hand." I couldn't resist; I nudged my lover and hissed, "I never knew Roderick was gay." At that precise moment there came a great shaking of the tree branches overhead, and some kind of nut hurled down and pinged me on the head! The Runesayer's way of letting me know he'd overheard my joke. So fare thee well, my kinsman and my friend. Save a place in the mead hall for me . . .

Saging Ritual . . . An Elder's Rite of Passage

Gather in some wild place by a water's edge, in praise of a worthy man who has given much to his community. This is one who has long imparted wisdom, lent vision to those coming after him, and striven hard to follow where the gods have led. His gifts to those he loves are many: his keen insight and intuition, his struggle for integrity and justice, his being in the turning of the seasons the wise counselor who binds hearts and hands together and the reaper who severs what he must, so that new seeds may spring up from burned and barren ground.

This is not his coming of age, for that happened years ago. This is rather the honoring of the fullness of his life, the conferring of his status as elder, sage, mage, or rank appropriate to his tradition. Elemental celebrants will gift and bless the sage, as his journey guides him to them.

The space is cleared with sacred smoke and ocean tides. One who bears an abalone shell and fragrant resin burning walks the circle round, intoning:

> "By sacred smoke we now invoke
> The blessings of this place.
> Let no one harm, let none alarm
> Its sanctity and grace."

One who carries a clear vessel containing seawater dips a small pine branch into it and sprinkles the circle area, saying:

> "Peace of the starlit waters,
> Peace of the briny deep.
> Blest are the sons and daughters,
> Whom ancient rites still keep."

The circle space has now been blessed with air and fire, water and earth. Celebrants take their place in circle through the eastern gate. The sage stands at the center, waiting. The eldest male in circle offers simple elemental invocations to the spirits of the place.

> **North:** "We call to the spirits of twilight. You whose purple shadows draw us deep into the Mystery, we seek your presence here."

People respond, "They come!"

> **East:** "We call to the keepers of sun, moon, and stars. You who hold the heavens at the dawning of the day, we seek your presence here."

People respond, "They come!"

> **South:** "We call to the crimson rays of noonday bright. You from whom nothing can hide, we seek your presence here."

People respond, "They come!"

> **West:** "We call to the bottomless deep. You who are the darkness, sweet repose, we seek your presence here."

People respond, "They come!"

The eldest guides the sage to the north, where Priest and Priestess await. The Priest stands staff in hand, the Priestess is cloaked. The Priest places his hands lightly on the sage's shoulders, looks into his eyes, and says:

> "Many times you have walked this circle, in lifetimes before and those that will come after. This round is most solemn, your journey of acknowledgement before the brothers and sisters of the Craft that you have pledged to serve. It is the blessing of the God and Goddess to whom you have dedicated your lifetime and your quest. At journey's end you will stand once more before us, changed forevermore, and utter the name by which you shall be known in this new incarnation among us. Are you ready to begin?"

The sage affirms that he is. The Priestess removes her cloak and fastens it about the sage's shoulders. She kisses him, saying, "The love of the Old Ones guide your way."

The Priest hands his staff to the sage, saying, "Wisdom and strength be your companions on the journey."

The eldest steps forward and guides the sage to the east, where fog is billowing (a bowl of dry ice and water, ringed by candles, will suffice). The Keepers of the East step forward and greet the sage.

One says:

> "Long are the nights you have sought the Mystery. Hard won have been your glimpses of beauty, power, and truth. Those gleanings you have carried to your people, granting them eyes to see, hearts to know, and courage to face what lies ahead. Your quest has not been in vain. We honor you as the seer, he who parts the mist. Accept this gift in token and remembrance. Blessed be!"

The sage is gifted with a small scrying mirror, perhaps with a pouch he may wish to tie to the cord at his waist, and is embraced.

The eldest next guides the sage to the south, where the distant sounds of hammering on metal can be heard, beyond the fire that blazes there. The different thickness and types of metal produce an eerie dwarven percussion as he approaches. One Keeper of the Flame steps forth to greet the sage; others continue to hammer.

The Keeper says:

> "Long have you fought to see justice done. Fierce has been your battle, and thankless it seemed at times. We say it is not so. Like the sword that is forged of searing heat, struck down a thousand times before it cools, so your spirit has been strengthened and made stronger, more resilient. How you gleam in our eyes, a bold beacon! We behold you as the Warrior, who defends what must remain and cleaves what cannot be. Accept

now this blade, in honor and in courage. Blessed
be!"

The sage holds out his hands to receive the blade and is gifted,
then embraced. The eldest walks him to the west, where waters
murmur. The Keepers of the Water step forth.

One says:

"In many guises you are Lover to us all. Your heart
and arms have opened wide, to take us in. You
have been shelter, protector, brother, and friend.
Your passion has kindled the spark when our own
faith has failed. Your hands have been ever the
first to bless, console, and heal. You have offered
of yourself and of your visions; been counselor,
priest, and guide at times when our own hopes
grew dim. Accept now this gift in gratitude and
love. Blessed be!"

A vial of magical oil is used to anoint the sage's brow, and is
then given to him. He is embraced long and earnestly by the
Keepers of the West.

Finally, the eldest walks with the sage back to the north,
where the Priest and Priestess wait. The Priest nods his head
solemnly to the sage, meets his eyes, and says:

"Welcome now, our brother—anointed, loved, and
blessed. We honor you as Guardian, and charge you
to ever be watchful of that which must remain.
Will you swear thus?"

The sage affirms. They embrace.

The Priestess unclasps a medallion from around her own
neck, and fastens it around that of the sage, saying:

"You are a jewel among us, and honored for your wisdom, your compassion, and the service you have given to these children of the gods. Will you swear that it shall ever be thus?"

The sage affirms. They embrace.

The Priest beckons all the guests and elementals to draw near. The Priest removes the antlered crown from his own brow and places it on that of the sage, saying, "This day we have honored the greatest of men, our own _____ [*name of seeker*], whom now we greet as elder of the Craft." Turning to the sage, the Priest asks, "By what name shall we know you now?"

If the sage has selected a new elder name, he now speaks it. All assembled shout, "Welcome, _____, and blessed be!"

The Priestess says, "May this journey end in gladness and rejoicing. Come share this simple feast and blessed be!" Cakes and ale follow.

After a suitable time of feasting and rejoicing, the circle must be closed. The people assemble once again, this time with the sage standing with the Priest and Priestess in the north.

It is the sage who now dismisses the quarters widdershins, thusly:

North: "Spirits of the twilight, we are wrapped in your presence and led by your beckoning hand. As you depart to your own fair realms, our love goes ever with you."

People respond, "Go in peace and blessed be!"

West: "You whose dark arms encircle the world, keep us ever in your embrace. As you depart to your own fair realms, our love goes ever with you."

People respond, "Go in peace and blessed be!"

South: "Keepers of noonday bright, grant we walk always in brilliance and honor. As you depart to your own fair realms, our love goes ever with you."

People respond, "Go in peace and blessed be!"

East: "You who light our way, grant us ever your silver grace and the glimpse of a guiding star. As you depart to your own fair realms, our love goes ever with you."

People respond, "Go in peace and blessed be!"

The Priest and Priestess turn widdershins, saying:

"We now release what once was bound, mundane realms from sacred ground. The circle is open, yet magic spins, for we carry the love of the gods within.

Farewell, and blessed be. This rite is done."

Prayer to the Sun God

It was springtime in San Francisco, and nights were foggy and cold. I had been sent by the university where I worked to attend a weeklong seminar hosted by the University of San Francisco, and I couldn't wait to get home and be warm. In the dorm room, only one socket of the pole lamp worked; the other two dangled limply and had blind eyes. One scant blanket was distributed per room, so thin I could hold it up and see the skyline through it. The phone was out of order for the first five days. When a friend finally did get through, her first words were, "Did you know that your phone extension is 666?!" Yup, somehow I suspected.

I cheered myself up with walks through the Haight-Ashbury and down Divisadero Street, where quaint metaphysical shops were discovered. I packed my pockets with seed pods from campus trees, snitched a flower here and there, and arranged a tiny altar atop the dorm room dresser. My contra-band votive candle, furtively lit a few moments each day in that nonsmoking facility, quickly burned to a nub.

On my last day there I called for an airport shuttle and was told that because of the rains and thickening fog, flights might be cancelled that day. My heart sank. I went back to my dorm room to pack last-minute things and took a second to light the last of my candle. Stepping to the window, I peered out into the drizzle and gloom and said:

"Lord Apollo, Golden One. I have never worked with you before, and I do not know you well. But if you could please hear me now . . . I long to go back home. Could you please clear the skies and let me pass through? My thanks for any aid you might lend."

The shuttle arrived, and a soaking wet Antonio tossed my bags inside. As we took off down the road, another shuttle from a rival company pulled up abreast of us. Antonio and the other young driver honked their horns, shook their fists at one another, and exchanged heated insults in a foreign tongue! What the—?!

He saw my consternation and, throwing his dark head back, laughed raucously. Then he winked and shared the joke. "That is my friend from the old country," he explained, dark eyes twinkling. "He is not long here. We make fun. His name is Apollo."

At that moment the sky cleared and the sun came shining through. I kid you not. The Sun God heard my prayer and answered it in person. I've never had a smoother flight . . .

Croning Ritual

Each woman on the Crone path is different. Some are solemn, others ribald. Some let 'er rip and speak their minds; others hold their quiet authority. I've not attended a Croning or had one myself. I've only heard tales of Wise Womyn friends' regal, stately Cronings. I've watched the videotape of my sister-in-law's Croning, where she was challenged by three horrible hags—of sexual decline, physical decay, and death—and had to confront them and emerge victorious. Eeek!

I envision a milder, more celebratory Croning. Depending on weather, time of year, and preference, this ceremony may be held outdoors in a garden, or indoors in a special room prepared for this purpose. Flowers are in great profusion, real or silk, and strands of tiny purple lights twine twinkling all around. Lavender incense or the Crone's favorite fragrance is burning, and her favorite Goddess/Crone hymn is playing either live or by boom box as she is escorted in.

Two Maidens walk at her side, and lead her to the throne prepared in her honor. This may be as inventive as a white wicker garden chair draped with purple tulle and flowers or an actual velvety overstuffed chair, with an orchid-colored throw. Let your budget, imagination, and meanderings through thrift shops be your guide. You may wish to gift the throne to the Crone for her home, or if she is part of a coven that could host future Croning rituals, reserve the throne for that purpose. Guests of all ages are seated in a semicircle around her. The Crone seats herself and the music ends.

The one facilitating this ritual, who should be a Crone herself, steps forth and says, "Today, we honor _____, whose footsteps led her lightly down the Maiden's way. With caution and care, her feet found the path paved by the Mother. She next looked around and sought the many roads chosen by the Empress, and selected the one that was true to her heart. Now, at last, _____ has come to the place of the Wise Woman, the Crone. We honor her journey and rejoice at the wisdom, spirit, and richness she brings us. _____, we love and honor you this day! Blessed be _____!"

All those gathered repeat, " _____, we love and honor you this day! Blessed be _____!"

The Maidens step forth, one of them asking, "As a Maiden, what song did you sing?"

The Crone replies, "My Maiden song was _____." She names a song, preselected, that she feels typifies her young life, her spirit, or her path. It is played for her, and those in attendance sing along. At the end of the song, one of the Maidens clasps an amethyst necklace chosen with care around the Crone's throat, and says, "You have made our hearts rejoice and our spirits sing. We gift you with _____." (She describes the necklace and its magical attributes.)

Both Maidens say, " _____, we love and honor you this day! Blessed be _____!"

All those gathered repeat, " _____, we love and honor you this day! Blessed be _____!"

Two women of Mother phase step forward. One of them asks the Crone, " _____, as a Mother, in what did you find courage, strength, and love?" The Crone replies, and reads a poem she has either written or found, in honor of that portion of her life. When she has finished, the other Mother steps forth and bids the Crone stand. A purple cloak or stole is draped about her shoulders, and the Mother says, "Your heart has wrapped around our lives and blessed those you have loved. Your courage is a shield and a protection. You honor us with your strength. Let us likewise wrap you, in praise and high regard."

Both Mothers say, " _____, we love and honor you this day! Blessed be _____!"

All those gathered repeat, " _____, we love and honor you this day! Blessed be _____ !"

Two women of middle-aged Empress phase step forth. One of them asks the Crone: " _____, did you dance for freedom and for joy?" The Crone replies "Yes," and a preselected piece of music, one of her favorites to dance to, is played. The Crone rises from her throne, guests join her, and they dance to her tune. (If because of physical limitations or mobility restrictions, the Crone cannot dance, guests gather around her and dance in her honor.)

When the music has ended, all take their seats again. One of the Empresses places a special garland or headdress on the Crone's head, saying to her, " _____, we celebrate your wildness and your passion! Never forget that the Wild Woman and the Wise Woman are twins."

Both Empresses say, " _____, we love and honor you this day! Blessed be _____!"

All those gathered repeat, " _____, we love and honor you this day! Blessed be _____!"

Finally, two women of Crone phase step forth. One of them asks the new Crone: " _____, in what have you found magic?" The new Crone answers, briefly describing her talents, teachings, and legacy.

The second Crone then asks her, " _____, are you ready to receive the tokens of power?" The new Crone affirms that she is, and rises. One Crone hands her a staff crafted especially for her. It may be draped or painted in her colors, and set with stones, tinkling bells, fur, and feathers. That Crone says, "_____, may you ever walk with honor." The second Crone presents a drum, painted with sigils, runes, or images sacred to the new Crone, saying, " _____, may your voice ever be heard."

Both Crones say, " _____, we love and honor you this day! Blessed be _____!"

All those gathered repeat, "_____, we love and honor you this day! Blessed be _____!"

The one facilitating now comes forth and asks, "Wise Woman, by what name shall we know you now?" If the Crone has chosen a new magical name for this phase of her journey, she divulges it at this point. The facilitator bids the Crone rise, kisses her, and anoints her brow with sacred oil. She and the new Crone then turn to face the guests, and the facilitator announces, "Children of the Goddess, I bring you _____. She is a new Crone among you, fairest jewel in the Lady's crown. Respect her for her wisdom, seek her for her stories, warm your souls by her fire. _____ [*new name*], we love and honor you this day! Blessed be _____!"

All those gathered repeat, "_____, we love and honor you this day! Blessed be _____ !"

The facilitator then signals people forth to lend their congratulations, embraces, and well-wishes. A reception may follow.

Annette's Buffet

Some say that to be born with a caul, or a veil, is to possess the gift of second sight. Others say it presages an extraordinary destiny. Medieval midwives used to wipe away, with a piece of paper, the wisp of amniotic sac still covering a newborn's face. The paper was then tucked carefully into an envelope, sealed, and given to the mother as a powerful talisman. Fishermen swore that possessing a caul saves one from drowning at sea. Roman statesmen carried a caul on their person, for it was said to bestow upon the bearer wisdom, honor, and psychic powers. Lord Byron, Liberace, Queen Christina of Sweden, and Alexander the Great all entered the world this way. So did Grandmother Annette.

As a young girl in Sweden, accompanying lovestruck chums to fortune tellers, Annette only knew that she always came away disappointed. "We can tell you nothing!" the oracle would say, shaking her head. "The only one who knows your future is you!" Annette was always tiny, too small for her Swedish father to give her a middle name. "She is so little . . . let her earn her first name before she gets a second one," he had said. She married her sweetheart Bror at age sixteen; a few years later, they came to America.

I met her on the day I married her grandson, generations later. Annette walked up and hugged me, barely coming to my shoulders. Then she turned to my mother and said, "We have to share her now. This one used to be mine." We grew tightly bonded. Annette would step to the phone to call me, just as my car pulled into her drive. There were no secrets from Annette. She proclaimed family joys before they were announced and pronounced the cause of sorrow before it was confessed.

I loved her dearly, she and Bror. My husband and I had standing card-playing dates with them. Before the deck was shuffled, out came tiny crystal shot glasses from an antique hutch. A swallow of wine was poured into each, so that we might "toast our worthy opponents." Glasses clinked together and all exclaimed, "Skål!"

During breaks to tally scores, coffee—brewed with eggshells to absorb any bitterness—was served. Annette's apologetic "We haven't a crumb in the house" usually turned into three kinds of cheese, imported sausage, and a wonderfully crispy bread called *rusk*.

When my husband and I were newlyweds, scrimping and scavenging furniture, Bror and Annette called and asked if we could use a dining room set. You bet! Eagerly we accepted the dining room table and chairs and a buffet. For the seven years of my first marriage, I cherished those pieces, especially Annette's buffet. Family photos, my candle altar, birthday gifts from one I loved—all came to rest there. Then when my spouse and I divorced, I relinquished the furniture back to his line. I told myself that if there ever were a chance, I'd give the world just to have Annette's buffet.

My former mate went on to marry and divorce a second time. Annette and her sweetheart Bror grew old and died within a year of one another. Many years went by before I was sent a dream. I walked one night, on the astral, through the second wife's basement. In the outer room, I could discern the dining room table and chairs, but no buffet. Then I glimpsed its shadowy silhouette in the smaller room that adjoined. A folded note card sat perched atop the buffet. I picked it up in the hazy light and read in familiar script, "For you, from the gods, with blessings."

Not long after, my daughter got a call. Would she like that old furniture of her dad's grandparents? Angela's stepmother asked. He had no place to put it, and the second ex wanted new. "Um . . . maybe," Ang replied, and immediately called me up. "Grab it!" I told her excitedly. "That buffet is mine!"

Because my son-in-law Kevin was getting out of the Navy, and headed with Ang and their son for civilian life in Phoenix, the Navy packed up the furniture back in Illinois and shipped it to Arizona. With the unveiling came a plot twist that no one could foresee. I held my breath as movers huffed and puffed and shoved the crate upstairs into my apartment. Nails were pried away, boards were stacked to the side, and an imposter stood revealed in my living room. I'd never laid eyes on that buffet before! There had surely been some mix-up or substitution, and I was devastated.

Two days later, the explanation came, and it's a marvel. Angela called her father, who disclosed that the buffet he and I had owned had actually come from aged neighbors of Bror and Annette's, who were moving and selling off furniture. They knew that we newlyweds could use whatever they could give, and so that beloved buffet came to dwell with us. It never was Annette's, and through the course of years it has wound up with my former sister-in-law, who loves it as much as I did.

As for the mystery sent to me, yes, it truly was Annette's. Purchased soon after they arrived in America, it held a special place of honor in her heart and in her home. I cherish it, too. How she heard my prayer from beyond the grave, I will never know. But mornings I light a candle and thank the ancestors who smile down from photo frames on the wall above her buffet. Bror and Annette are there, too.

Paying Tribute

In my small hometown newspaper there is a special section for donations around the holiday times. One reads notes about Christmas baskets, in memory of a loved one no longer living. It's a wonderful sentiment, and I've sent in contributions from the kids and me on past occasions.

Can we honor the memory of those departed we hold dear, and nourish our community at the same time? I think it's quite possible. Please remember that this idea comes from only one Witch, and that if you adopt it and make it your own, the tradition can become whatever you make it.

Here is how it takes shape in my home. On my kitchen counter there sits a small orange teapot. When it arrived via mail order, it was smaller than I envisioned; it might only be big enough to serve tea to a handful of mice. However, it holds the few extra dollar bills left over at the end of my pay period quite nicely when I fold the bills, tuck them inside, and forget them. I do this as frequently as I can throughout the year, and try my darnedest not to borrow money back.

Each year, just after Samhain, I choose the person whose name I shall gift in. If their birthday is known, the gift will be given on that date after a year has passed. If unknown to me, I choose a month for which they had a fondness. My friend Barbi loved Beltane most of all. A white-haired mage named Chyron always made me think of Father Christmas and of Yule. My Aunt Edna was a June gal. You get the idea.

Then I consider what work appealed to each. Barbi was an herbalist, so I sign up for online newsletters from herb shops in town. If there's a class of interest to me that has a registration fee, I pay it from my teapot hoard and attend, in memory of her. I obtain the teacher's contact information and send a thank-you note a week after the class. I express appreciation to the teacher for the chance to learn, and write a couple of lines about my friend Barbi and how she would have gained a lot from the class as well.

Chyron was an inventor, always tinkering with something or other and coming up with all manner of odd gadgets that always inexplicably worked. In his honor, I might count the cash I've saved up, call a local vocational school for contact specifics, and mail in a donation to cover small parts or lab supplies.

For the Pagan authors who have passed, let us sustain those bookstore owners who carry their works. Take your gifting money and buy a couple copies of the work that inspired you most. Give one to a Pagan event's raffle and the other to a study group. The magic and the legacy live on.

Autumn

Autumn is a whisper on the wind,
Autumn is the longing for a friend . . .

September

October

November

December

gift from the gods

January

February

March

April

May

June

July

August

Yule Log Lighting Invocation

We ignite the Fire of Inspiration.
At this time when night is longest
And life may seem uncertain,
May each of us seek the inner glow
Of Truth, Creativity,
Courage, and Compassion.
May we become the Light.
We fan the Flames of Wonder!
In this Season of the Child,
May each one of us
Continue to marvel at life!
Joy is in the air,
And miracles come wrapped in Everyday.
May we never grow too old to sing, dance,
Share our stories and adventures,
Laugh and remember to play!
We call into being the Spark of Rebirth.
As Nature ever renews herself,
And seasons and cycles turn,
Likewise may we also
Transcend, evolve,
And continue to grow.
Blessed be.

Not every gift comes wrapped with a shiny bow and a candy cane. While it is great to share in the presents and merrymaking that this month is all about, there is also a need for introspection—pulling back a bit and making a space for the gift of the gods that always unexpectedly comes. Perhaps in the midst of frantic shopping, there is a moment of humor, some ludicrous thing you will share with your friends and laugh about for many Yules to come. Maybe your tired feet and weary soul find sanctuary in some little park or spot of beauty off the beaten track, and it becomes your place of peace. Being in the right place at the right time in December leads to hearing and falling in love with a new musical artist, a previously undiscovered novelist, or a new passion or endeavor. The Yuletide has much to bestow, and we must allow ourselves to be the recipients as well. Whatever our beliefs, there are angels everywhere.

Decked in December's finest, you will find among these pages some packages just for you. Step up and claim your blessings, holding them securely in both hands. Cast away the bane and pains of the old year passing and leave spaces for the new year's blessings to fill. Lastly, you will find a sweet suggestion for getting out the cookie cutters and baking up a story. Glad Yule to one and all!

Claiming the Blessings

We are quick to rejoice with others when fortune smiles their way. We send cards of congratulation, roses of acknowledgement, and join in taking those so favored out to lunch in honor of achievement, good news, promotion, or other blessings. Yet when the gods lay something large and wondrous in our own laps, we shy away. Why is it that we deem others worthy of great goodness and are so reluctant to believe it of ourselves? We must open up our hands, take a deep breath and a leap of faith, and claim those blessings that have come our way. In the claiming comes the acceptance within us that *yes*, this beneficence is real. Yes, it really has been offered to you. No, the Universe did not get confused and deliver it to the wrong address. This is yours, you deserve it, and you get to keep it . . .

Go with another—a Priest or Priestess for whom you have mutual love and esteem—to accomplish this rite. Your needs will be simple: a circle of stone, big enough for just you to stand in. This symbolizes the barrier of self-doubts and fears that keep you from claiming the blessing. The one performing this ritual with you will need sage and a smudge fan, blessing oil for anointing, and a pouch containing crushed herbs, fine glitter, and so forth. This is the visual "blessing." Also take a bottle of good wine or sparkling cider and two goblets, to celebrate the providence afterward.

The Priest or Priestess smudges the area to be used, saying aloud, "We ask blessings of the stones, guardians of the earth, to serve as boundary and release. We ask blessings of the waters to carry the blessings from the womb of the Great Mother, into the hands of _____, and to carry away all doubts and insecurities. We ask the spirits of air and fire to cleanse and sanctify this place. May it be a fitting temple for the claim-

gift from the gods

ing of blessings. So mote it be." Lastly, the one to be blessed is smudged and purified.

You and your clergy now create your circle of stones. When this is done, stand facing the Priest or Priestess, who says to you, "_____, you have built a fortress to keep benevolence out. What good is a wall, when it shields you from joy, fulfillment, and prosperity that is yours? What is it that prevents you?"

You speak of what separates you from that which has come to you, and the reasons for your hesitation. There are no special words here, other than the ones that pour forth from your heart.

Your clergy hears your words, considers them, and asks clarifying questions if need be. Then when you have finished, he or she says, "I bid you now transform your wall into a path, to set your feet on the road to joy, to guide you toward acceptance of this miracle meant for you alone."

Open one end of your stone circle, the end facing the Priest or Priestess, so that it becomes an open semicircle, instead of an enclosed round.

The clergy says, "_____, are you ready to step forth? Will you accept the gift of the gods that has been given, and claim it on this day? Will you receive your due?"

Affirm that you are prepared to do this and step forth, out of the now-opened stone circle.

The clergy anoints your brow, saying, "_____, favored of the gods, I honor the courage you have found within you. The Old Ones smile on you this day." He or she bids you hold out your hands.

The clergy takes the pouch and pours the wonderful mix of fragrant herbs and shimmery stuff into your hands, saying, "Good fortune has come to you. Let your heart and hands be glad. What is this blessing that has come into your life?"

gift from the gods

Speak from your heart of the good thing that has come your way.

The clergy asks, "_____, are you ready to accept this as truly being yours, and meant for you alone?" You affirm that this is so. Clergy then bids you, "Now celebrate your happiness and let joy engulf you like a wind!"

Fling the handfuls of blessing upward into the air, so that they cascade all over you as they drift back down. One can never have too many rose petals or too much faery dust, you know.

This is the moment to sing, shout, whoop, and dance around. Then you crack open that bottle of wine or cider, and toast to the wonderful thing that you so richly deserve.

A Glimpse Through Angel Eyes

"Bronwynn, do you smell smoke?" my good friend Ali wrinkled her nose. The hour was late and the children had long gone to bed, that week before Christmastime. I sniffed the air, shook my head. She and I sat talking the hours away as snow piled up outside. Then Ali paused. "There it is again. I'm smelling burning wood." I assured her 'twas just someone's fireplace, stoked up against the Illinois wintertime cold, but I put on my coat and went outside. Wind stung my cheeks as I turned all around, trying to pick up a scent on the wind. I could detect nothing, anywhere. I went back inside.

And thus it went on, for an hour more, with that elusive hint of smoke, wafting like a ghost through the air. I went from room to room, checking out appliances, sockets, finding nothing. Finally, I bundled up again, went back outside. This time, I closed my eyes, trying to hone in on just the sense of smell and nothing else. Suddenly, my mind's eye was filled with the image of a radiant face. A golden glow shone through him, flooded all around him. A being of light I realized: an angel, older than Christian and Pagan alike. Then without opening his mouth, he spoke. "You must search the darkness," the being said to me. Then he was gone.

I flung open the door, hurled myself inside, and frantically began flipping off lights. Ali thought I had lost my mind. "Humor me!" I snapped, as I ran from room to room. There in my eight-year-old daughter's room, I felt my knees go week. Ang, preferring to sleep with a light on, had removed the shade from her lamp. It sat on her dresser, shoved up against the paneled wall. A huge angry red arc glowed around the bulb, where it had burned its way into the wood! I never saw it when the lights were on, but here it was plainly visible in the dark. "You must search the darkness," he had said.

Ali scooped Ang up and bedded her down on the living room couch. I feverishly raced to the sink and soaked towels with water, pressing them sopping against the wall again and again. The glowing sphere darkened and turned to black. I phoned the rural fire department and waited to hear their sirens scream through the frosty dawn. Everything was checked, the fire was out, and damage was minimal.

Who or what would've been left standing, had I not "searched the darkness," is a sobering thought indeed. Ang knows beyond a doubt that she has a guardian angel, and a handsome one at that. She figures he draws overtime pay, just looking out for her. As for me, the gift of life arrived just a few days before Christmas . . . a glimpse through an angel's eyes.

A Casting of Stones at Year's End

For some, it has been an arduous year. Here, then, is a releasing ritual, designed to make peace with all this year has wrought. Let us unburden ourselves, so that we may embrace the coming year and all of its changes with gladness.

Go you into a quiet place, and take with you these things: the makings of a small contained fire, frankincense and myrrh, a charcoal block and thurible, a chalice with wine or juice, and a white jar candle. Plastic milk jugs make excellent shields against the wind. Cut the top part open wider, leaving the carrying handle. Pack a little loose dirt in the bottom and set your charcoal block in one and your jar candle in the other.

Take a bag of stones. These should not be pretty or pleasing stones, as they symbolize the hardships of the year. Take also an offering for the spirits of the land; bread crumbs or a seed ball to hang from an accommodating tree branch would be welcome here.

Clear a space, kindle your fire, and say as sparks ignite, "I build the funeral pyre of sadness and despair. Here is the death of sorrow. Like the Phoenix, I rise anew."

Light your incense and savor the fragrance, saying, "Blessings have come on the wind . . . the sound of laughter, the scent of joy. I hold these things in memory, for hope is a precious thing and casts out doubt and fear."

Fill your chalice with wine or juice and pour forth a libation on the ground, saying:

> "To the Lord and Lady, I offer the contents of my
> heart. Although at times my heart has bled, and I
> have felt weary or alone, I have known kindness,
> too. For those cared, who lent willing aid, I give
> blessing and thanks."

Light the candle, saying, "Lady of renewal and compassion, Horned One of both tenderness and strength, I stand before you now. The old year ends and the new one just begins. Many are the blessings which have come." Speak of all that for which your heart is glad.

Shake out the bag of stones upon your altar space, saying, "There have been heartaches, too." Pick up one stone, saying, "I name you the time of _____ [*list the specific hardship*], and I cast you away from me!" Then hurl the stone into the distance, as far as the eye can see. Continue doing this until all of your grief has been named and your stones are gone.

Take up the chalice, saying, "I raise the cup in honor of my gods." Speak honest words of praise to those deities you follow. "May they ever guide me on my way. Blessed be!"

Next, raise the cup to yourself, saying, "I toast to the man/woman that I am, one of _____ ." List truthfully those good traits and talents you possess. "In all the world, there is none like me. In my eyes is the reflection of the gods." Drink to yourself.

Lastly, state, "In the names of the Old Ones, I declare that I am free. I open my mind to possibilities. I open my heart to those who would show me love. I open my soul to fulfill my destiny. Let my journey begin. So mote it be!"

Leave your offering to the spirits of the place, asking their blessing and protection upon your coming year. Listen quietly for bits of inner wisdom, then move on . . .

Baking Up the Story

Cookie cutters are marvelous things, and you can find them in every shape and size. When I was a kid, my mom had a large metal canister full of cutters of many kinds. There were bells and Scottie dogs, a fire truck and a star, cookie cutter numbers, gingerbread men and hearts. Far too many to count, and when we baked up Christmas cookies I could guess which cutters had been used the most and which were barely broken in.

Storytelling is gaining renewed interest as a hearth-fire, time-honored art. Why not fit it to your child's circumstance and imagination and bake cookies to tell the tale? Is your family going to face changes sometime in the coming year? Help your youngster pick cutters in the shapes of things he or she hopes to find. Perhaps one shaped like a schoolhouse might symbolize a new school district, or moving up a grade. Find a cutter shaped like a truck to represent the family van and hand your kiddo a toothpick. Let him draw in his face, looking eagerly out the window as you explore the new neighborhood.

If your little one has to miss some school due to sickness or surgery, wait until your child is up walking and starting to fidget, then bake a story to make them well. A grandfather living in Texas might become the cowboy hero of this fanciful, edible tale. Find a cookie cutter shaped like a star, for his badge. He'll need a horse to ride when he goes after the bank robbers, right? Dig out the horse-shaped cutter, and maybe one shaped like a bag. Let your child trace dollars on it, and you've got "the loot."

If your child is more into princesses, castles, and faeries, you can find those cookie cutters too. Some online research has convinced me there are cookie cutter clubs, just like the old recipe exchange ones.

Between you and your wee one, brainstorm enough parts to the story to bake just the right amount of cookies—one for each day your kiddo has to miss school. The magic is in the making, so let the child use the cookie cutters and ice the cookies when they're cool. The prescription is one cookie a day, until your child is well. What a tasty cure!

To Sing in Harmony

In November of 1992, Z Budapest came to town. The famous Witch with the silver-spiked hair was scheduled to present a book signing and lecture at a Phoenix New Age shop. My daughter Ang and I, both ardent fans, pounced on tickets and anxiously waited for the date to roll around. Folks queued up to have their favorites of Z's books signed. Ang and I were overjoyed that, unlike some austere celebrities, Z chuckled and hugged and was a warm-hearted Hungarian delight.

The lecture on the Goddess and her Consort ended and a hundred people rose from chairs to form a circle. Suddenly Ang gasped and elbowed me. "Mom, she's here!" Ang whispered. "Oh my gosh, Mom, Lisa's here!" Sure enough, there stood my long-estranged friend, glaring across at me. The situation that had ripped apart our friendship had been sudden and stupid but had caused irreparable damage. What to do? Should I approach? What horrible things might she say to me?

Hand to hand, a candle was passed and each holder spoke his or her name aloud and voiced what they'd ask that energy be sent toward. Surprisingly, Lisa asked for healing. I gathered my courage and when the candle came to me, I quietly said, "Understanding." Blessings were spoken, chants were sung, then came a silent lull.

Soft at first, then growing in volume, Lisa began to sing. She chose a Pagan ballad whose verses speak of anger, misconceptions, and the need to uncover the truth. I joined her on the chorus, with others in circle now singing along. Energy flowed between us, clean and pure and whole.

How lovely, from such discord, to sing in harmony . . .

Light Prayer

Seek the Light
Share the Light
Shine the Light
Become the Light!
Blessed be!

Conclusion

To those who stir the sparks and keep our faith alive, I am honored to have had this occasion to warm my hands by your fire. Keep that kettle on the hearth and a candle in the window, and let's talk again soon . . .

Old Ones bless,
Bronwynn Forrest Torgerson

Free Magazine

Read unique
articles by Llewellyn
authors, recommendations by experts,
and information on new releases. To receive a **free** copy of
Llewellyn's consumer magazine, *New Worlds of Mind &*
Spirit, simply call 1-877-NEW-WRLD or visit our website
at www.llewellyn.com and click on *New Worlds.*

LLEWELLYN ORDERING INFORMATION

Order Online:
Visit our website at www.llewellyn.com, select your books, and order them on
our secure server.

Order by Phone:
- Call toll-free within the U.S. at 1-877-NEW-WRLD
  (1-877-639-9753). Call toll-free within Canada at
  1-866-NEW-WRLD (1-866-639-9753)
- We accept VISA, MasterCard, and American Express

Order by Mail:
Send the full price of your order (MN residents add 7% sales tax) in
U.S. funds, plus postage and handling to:

> Llewellyn Worldwide
> 2143 Wooddale Drive, Dept. 978-0-7387-1369-4
> Woodbury, MN 55125-2989, U.S.A.

Postage and Handling:

Standard (U.S., Mexico, and Canada). If your order is:
> $24.99 and under, add $3.00
> $25.00 and over, FREE STANDARD SHIPPING

AK, HI, PR: $15.00 for one book plus $1.00 for
each additional book.

International Orders (airmail only):
> $16.00 for one book plus $3.00 for each additional book

Orders are processed within two business days.
Please allow for normal shipping time. Postage and handling rates subject to change.

The Real Witches' Handbook

A Complete Introduction to the Craft

KATE WEST

What is a real Witch? With honesty and friendly flair, Kate West sets the record straight about the life of a modern Witch. Dispelling common myths and Hollywood-inspired images, she reveals the true beliefs and practices of this nature-oriented spirituality. Discover how the Witches' moral code is tied to respect for nature and animals, environmental responsibility, and the Wiccan Rede. Explore Sabbat celebrations, magic, divination, pathworking, and herb lore—and get a taste of the Witch's life with actual spells, rituals, meditations, and other activities.

From choosing a Witch name to initiation into the Craft, beginners will find everything they need here to take that first step onto an ancient Pagan path.

ISBN-13: 978-0-7387-1375-5

208 pages $15.95

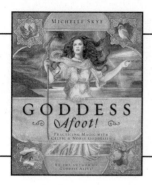

Goddess Afoot!

Practicing Magic with Celtic & Norse Goddesses

MICHELLE SKYE

Written in the same warm, practical style as *Goddess Alive!*, this book takes you further along on your spiritual path to the Goddess. With this guide, you'll discover how to use spellwork and magic to make lasting changes in your life. You'll learn how to attune to a specific goddess for inspiration and empowerment, and connect with the energy of that goddess to manifest your dreams and desires.

Each chapter starts with a goddess from the Norse or Celtic pantheons, and presents her myths, a pathworking, a guided meditation, an invocation, and three magical activities or crafts. Twelve powerful goddesses offer assistance in a variety of ways, from helping you attract abundance to becoming more psychic. You can gain balance in your life with Cymidei Cymeinfoll, the Welsh goddess of war and birth; learn to take risks with Cessair, the founding goddess of Ireland; and allow yourself to shine with Sunna, the Norse goddess of the sun.

ISBN 13: 978-07387-1331-1

288 pages $19.95

Summoning the Fates

A Guide to Destiny and Sacred Transformation

Zsuzsanna E. Budapest

During the 1956 Hungarian revolution, Z Budapest narrowly escaped a massacre. Was it chance that spared her life, or destiny?

Budapest, a pioneer of the women's spirituality movement, introduces us to the three Fates who rule our lives. Not even the gods and goddesses can escape these raw forces of nature presiding over the past, present, and future. Budapest uses fairy tales, historical lore, and personal anecdotes to describe the three sacred sisters who are especially active during our thirty-year life cycles: Urdh (youth), Verdandi (adulthood), and Skuld (the crone years).

Want a taste of the cosmic soup bubbling in Fate's cauldron? Budapest also offers heartfelt advice, exercises, and rituals to help you connect with the Fates and embrace your own unique destiny.

ISBN 13: 978-0-7387-1083-9

288 pages $15.95

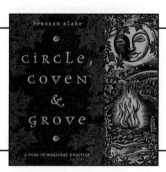

Circle, Coven & Grove
A Year of Magickal Practice

DEBORAH BLAKE

Green, Celtic, Alexandrian, Eclectic . . . every circle, coven, and grove of Witches is as unique as the magick they practice. No matter what kind of Witch you are, High Priestess Deborah Blake's guide to group practice has something for you.

An instruction manual, workbook, and Book of Shadows all rolled into one, *Circle, Coven & Grove* is an ideal tool for busy Witches, new groups, new leaders, groups sharing leadership, and Wiccans seeking inspiration for crafting rituals. Blake provides original—yet easy to modify—group rituals for New Moons, Full Moons, and Sabbats for a full Wheel of the Year. There are seasonal spells, blessings, and rituals for celebrating holidays, increasing energy, giving thanks, healing, and more. Blake also discusses circle etiquette and the dos and don'ts of establishing a group or becoming a group leader.

ISBN 13: 978-0-7387-1033-4

264 pages $14.95

Crafting Wiccan Traditions

Creating a Foundation for Your Spiritual Beliefs & Practices

RAVEN GRIMASSI

Eager to blaze your own Wiccan spiritual trail? Ready to express your own form of Divinity by crafting a tradition that's all your own? Raven Grimassi's comprehensive guide will help you merge your core Wiccan beliefs into a cohesive and transformative spiritual practice—a personalized path to the Divine.

Handpick a pantheon of harmonious deities. Customize your own rules and rituals. Incorporate existing myths or create your own. Perform magick? Choose a patron deity? Work with egregores? Keep a traditional Book of Shadows? It's up to you! Grimassi explores all modes of Wiccan worship and maps out key elements—gods and goddesses, ritual structure, religious / philosophical views, magical practices, coven structures, training, laws—to guide you through this soul-searching process.

Both solitary and group practitioners will discover how to anchor their new, eclectic tradition to a sound Wiccan foundation.

ISBN 13: 978-0-7387-1108-9

264 pages

$15.95

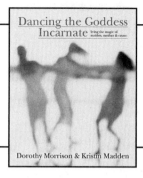

Dancing the Goddess Incarnate

Living the Magic of Maiden, Mother & Crone

Kristin Madden & Dorothy Morrison

Life is an adventure, a game, a dance. Whether you're shakin' it at the disco with Athena or doing the Charleston with Hecate, each goddess offers vital lessons for exploring—and enjoying—every facet of our lives.

No matter your age, *Dancing the Goddess Incarnate* can help you get in touch with the maiden, mother, and crone within. You don't have to know the rhythm or the steps. Simply allow each of the nine goddesses to lead you onto the dance floor outside your comfort zone, where you'll learn to unlock creativity, rediscover play, strategize success, and nurture yourself. This fun Pagan guide to self-exploration includes meditations, games, magic tips, herbal remedies, and exercises that can—with help from the goddesses—bring balance, beauty, and joy into your life.

Kristin Madden is the Dean of Ardantane's School of Shamanic Studies and has been a metaphysical and environmental educator for nearly twenty years.

Dorothy Morrison is a third-degree Wiccan High Priestess and has practiced the ancient arts for more than twenty-five years.

ISBN 13: 978-0-7387-0636-8

240 pages $14.95

To Ride a Silver Broomstick

New Generation Witchcraft

Silver RavenWolf

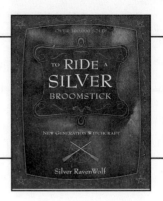

Throughout the world there is a new generation of Witches—people practicing or wishing to practice the Craft on their own, without an in-the-flesh magickal support group. *To Ride a Silver Broomstick* speaks to those people, presenting them with both the science and religion of Witchcraft, allowing them to become active participants while growing at their own pace. It is ideal for anyone: male or female, young or old, those familiar with Witchcraft and those totally new to the subject and unsure of how to get started.

Full of the author's warmth, humor, and personal anecdotes, *To Ride a Silver Broomstick* leads you step by step through the various lessons, with exercises and journal writing assignments. This is the complete Witchcraft 101, teaching you to celebrate the Sabbats, deal with coming out of the broom closet, choose a magickal name, visualize the Goddess and God, meditate, design a sacred space, acquire magickal tools, design and perform rituals, network, spellcast, perform color and candle magick, with instruction on divination, healing, telepathy, psychometry, astral projection, and much, much more.

ISBN 13: 978-0-8754-2791-1

320 pages $15.95

The Witch's Guide to Life

Kala Trobe

Some days it's not easy being a witch. Life is full of relationship problems, global crises, personal karmic drama . . . not to mention the challenge of practicing your craft in a nine-to-five world.

This comprehensive guide to magickal living spans the intellectual, physical, magickal, and philosophical aspects of a witch's life. It focuses on the history and development of modern Wicca; its core beliefs and practices; and magickal techniques such as successful spellcasting, aura reading, and Tarot and rune reading.

ISBN 13: 978-0-7387-0200-1

480 pages $19.95

A Year of Ritual

Sabbats & Esbats for Solitaries & Covens

SANDRA KYNES

It's easy to lose ourselves in the everyday business of life. One way to bring our bodies, minds, and spirits into alignment is through ritual celebrations. A vital part of Wicca and Paganism, ritual strengthens our connection to nature and helps us to enter the realm of the Divine.

For Witches and Pagans of all levels, *A Year of Ritual* provides ready-made rituals for a full year of Sabbats and Esbats. Groups or solitary participants can use these easy-to-follow rituals straight from the book. Ideas, words, and directions for each ritual are included along with background information, preparation requirements, and themes. This unique sourcebook also explains basic formats and components for creating your own rituals.

ISBN 13: 978-0-7387-0583-5

240 pages $14.95

The Witch's Coven

Finding or Forming Your Own Circle

EDAIN MCCOY

As a practicing solitary Witch, do you ever wonder what it's like to be a member of a coven . . . what happens at an initiation . . . how covens perform magick and healing?

Edain McCoy has been involved in Witchcraft for two decades. She wrote this book to answer all of these questions and more. Learn how a real Witch's coven operates, from initiation and secret vows to parting rituals. You'll get step-by-step guidance for joining or forming a coven, plus sage advice and exclusive insights to help you decide which group is the right one for you.

- Helps make the novice's entry into any coven easy and safe
- Explains the many different types of covens, so you can find the one that's right for you
- Shows established covens how to screen potential members and avoid common problems that hurt covens
- Provides ideas for organizing a teaching circle or mediating conflicts
- Contains a networking directory

ISBN 13: 978-0-7387-0388-6

224 pages $12.95

Women's Rites, Women's Mysteries

Intuitive Ritual Creation

RUTH BARRETT

How can women turn birthday parties, baby showers, and other rites of passage into empowering celebrations brimming with meaning and fiery feminine spirit?

Emphasizing the Dianic Wiccan tradition, Ruth Barrett shows women how they can create empowering, transformative rituals that strengthen their profound connection to the Goddess. Instead of providing shortcuts, scripts, or rote rituals, she teaches women how to think like a ritualist. Step by step, readers learn the ritual-making process: developing a purpose and theme, building an altar, preparing emotionally and mentally (energetics), spellcasting, and more. For beginners or experienced ritualists, solitaries or groups, this thorough, engaging guide to the art of ritual-making can help women commemorate every sacred milestone—from menstruation to marriage to menopause—that touches their lives.

ISBN 13: 978-0-7387-0924-6

312 pages $16.95

To order, call 1-877-NEW-WRLD

Prices subject to change without notice

L.A. Witch

Fiona Horne's Guide to Coven Magick

FIONA HORNE

Australia's favorite witch is now on our side of the globe! Leaving behind her successful life Down Under, Fiona Horne made the risky, exciting move to Los Angeles—a city of dreams and glamour—where she was inspired to form her first coven.

Bold, sassy, and utterly candid, *L.A. Witch* documents Fiona's enlightening journey from solitary to shared magickal practice. She makes it easy for beginners to follow in her footsteps by sharing the basics for starting a coven and enhancing it with personal flavor and flair. This lively introduction to the Craft also discusses Witchcraft history, Goddess spirituality, laws and ethics, rituals and spellwork, Wiccan sexuality, magickal excursions, and other fundamentals.

Topped off with diary entries, anecdotes, and Fiona's infectious personality, *L.A. Witch* brilliantly captures the extraordinary, magickal life of a coven Witch.

ISBN 13: 978-0-7387-1034-1

240 pages $14.95

Sexy Witch

LASARA FIREFOX

Employing a unique blend of feminism and magick, this refreshing guide to female self-empowerment helps women acknowledge the beauty, strength, and sexiness within themselves. Utterly honest and captivating, LaSara FireFox banishes the damaging misconceptions and shame often associated with female sexuality and sheds light on what it truly means to be a "Sexy Witch."

Each of the seven lessons—covering issues of body image, menstruation, genital exploration, self-acceptance, mentors, and gender—include fun facts, illuminating quotes, and exercises for nurturing the body and spirit. The second half of the book is devoted to rituals—to be practiced alone or with others—that celebrate one's power as a woman, a sexual being, and a Witch.

ISBN 13: 978-0-7387-0752-5

312 pages $14.95

Witch in the Boardroom

Proven Business Magic

STACEY DEMARCO

Must cutthroat tactics and backstabbing be synonymous with "getting ahead"? Does success in the corporate world equal spiritless, energy-draining drudgery? Successful business leader and experienced Witch Stacey Demarco insists that spirituality and business are not mutually exclusive. Combining Wiccan principles with down-to-earth business techniques, *Witch in the Boardroom* demonstrates how to rejuvenate your career and your spiritual life.

Demarco illustrates how to achieve material and spiritual fulfillment in the workplace by applying Witchcraft laws, spellworking, and magical thinking. Inspiring stories from the author's own case studies confirm the potency of the rituals and spells outlined in this Wiccan-based guide to business success.

ISBN 13: 978-0-7387-0840-9

312 pages $14.95